"This courageous story is also spiritual and inspiring. It's for those who need similar healing or those who want to delve more deeply into the ripple effects of sexual violence which is so prevalent in our society." —**Rev. Martin Padovani, SVD, author of** *Healing Wounded Emotions* **and** *Healing Wounded Relationships*

"*Divine Disclosure* gives a voice to the trauma endured by non-offenders, a long under-represented population, and it reveals a critical component lacking in today's conventional therapy: the spiritual healing of the soul." —**Amelia Sapio, LCSW-R, Dept. of Probation, Suffolk County, NY**

"Although buffeted by doubts and often paralyzed by fear, Janet Long emerges with an essential lesson for any trauma-tized person: No wound is beyond the healing touch of the Divine Physician, and no situation is too dark to respond to his balm of light and love. *Divine Disclosure* is a remarkable gift to a broken world." —**Genevieve Kineke, author and col-umnist, Feminine-genius.com**

"A friend told me a long time ago that sharing spiritual in-sights is like putting out a loaf of bread. Some people will take the entire loaf, some a few slices, others just crumbs. This book is like that loaf of bread. If you pick it up, you'll be fed." —**Rev. Martin F. McGeough, C.M., Former Coordinator, Jail and Prison Ministries, Diocese of Trenton, NJ**

DIVINE
DISCLOSURE

Spiritual Healing After Sexual Violence

Janet Long

To B.

"For out of much affliction and anguish of heart I wrote to you with many tears, not that you might be pained but that you might know the abundant love I have for you." (2 Corinthians 2:4)

These pages are also dedicated to~

Survivors who never told anyone

Perpetrators who think no one but the survivor knows what they've done

Parents, friends, and lovers of both these people

Survivors who told someone and then denied it all

People who listen to those they suspect might be survivors or offenders but say nothing

Friends of those who have sexually hurt others

Friends of those who have been hurt

Siblings of the survivor

Siblings of the perpetrator and the survivor in the same person

Co-workers of offenders

Students who have been offended against

Teachers, priests, military officers, and all others who offend

Doctors who suspect violence in relationships and don't ask about it

Children whose parents or relatives are offenders

Children whose parents are survivors

Spouses of survivors

Spouses of perpetrators

Spouses of both of these in the same person

Counselors, cops, neighbors, business owners, military members, and employees

Pastors, parents, anyone who has been hurt or who has harmed others sexually. Through God's grace, this is for you.

We are the innocent and the evil doers, the compromised, the takers and the complacent, the naïve and the negligent. We are souls in need of God's infinite mercy, which we receive through the truth of His Word Who is Jesus. When we bring Him an open heart—especially through the intercession of His Mother Mary, Most Pure—His mercy shall triumph in us.

Acknowledgements

Mary Ann was the first person to read a draft of this book. It was her encouragement that helped me believe I'd be shown a way to write about what I experienced and what I learned.

Genevieve and Barbara offered their financial support as well as their literary expertise, and it was crowned with wonderful care and support. Abby's skillful proofreading, editing suggestions, page formatting, and design were essential gifts to me. Donna and Amy offered thoughtful as well as practical input gleaned from their own professions. Endless thanks go to the many Sisters and Brothers in the Spirit who interceded on my behalf over the years of preparation and process needed to produce this book. I'm indebted to numerous diocesan priests and those from the order of the Franciscan Friars of the Primitive Observance in New England. Their healing prayer, compassion, and listening hearts have hopefully produced good fruit on these pages.

Through it all was the gentle presence and prayers of my mother, Ruth, who gifted me with a second birth. She gave me a safe home to write in and love to trust in as I healed. Gradually, we walked together to the end of her long and blessed life. If you see any courage or strength here, surely she is to be thanked for helping it bloom.

Table of Contents

Preface

In a recent workshop I attended for supporting families in sexual assault cases, there was a segment on a disorder called *vicarious traumatization* (VT). Learning that what I suffered had scientific validation seemed to strengthen my already significant belief in God's desire to heal us. Initially VT was thought to happen solely among counseling staff, but since 9/11, it's also being reported by clergy, first responders, and humanitarian workers. This book may be among the first to show the incidence of VT in family members. Its symptoms are like burnout or compassion fatigue, but the onset can emerge suddenly instead of over time. This was the case with me. Immediately after the disclosure of sexual assault in the family, the world as I knew it was changed and so was I.

Research notes that a person's susceptibility to the effects of VT may be due to their negative coping skills or by having a shared history of trauma with those they serve. From the outset I had no intentions of "coping" with the crimes committed, as social workers are expected to do. I wanted resolution. Nothing less. And if awareness of the crimes comes after the fact as it did in my case, there's little chance that the empathy factor won't be in the extreme. As for having a similar trauma history, the survivor and I shared the same roof with the perpetrator so there is little doubt there.

The most important feature of my brief introduction to VT was learning what is at its core. The heart of vicarious traumatization, experts say, is its spiritual effect. Research shows those who suffer from VT experience a deep affront to their spirituality as a result. There are feelings of a loss of meaning in their lives, a disconnection from others, and the dreadful belief that they are unworthy of love. VT doesn't subside until these compromised beliefs about the self and the world are worked through. The suggested treatment from experts is to deepen our spiritual lives with the aim of correcting these distortions.

The above symptoms correspond to conditions of *spiritual warfare* and *a crisis of faith*. The "remedy" for these is to seek transformative renewal in mind and soul from God's grace. This protocol aligns with those from the scientific community but uses a language and Source of supply that are spiritual and transcendent.

These findings support the experience of the spiritually wounded. Further, evidence that those who help in the healing of the traumatized may be wounded themselves in the process can be paralleled with the suffering servant in the book of Isaiah. This affords us a new vision. Instead of seeing our faith, indeed even our God as deficient in the struggle to heal after sexual violence, we can thank Him for His use of every good thing, including an alliance between faith and social science to join us in fighting the good fight. Our understanding of spiritual healing can no longer be vague. It is a magnificent gift from God available to anyone who truly wants it. May this book help spread that good news.

J. L.
May 2021

What This Book Is About

T his is the story of how God transforms us when we turn to Him in the aftermath of sexual violence. These pages are written to victims, perpetrators, and non-offenders because God loves each of us and has an abundant life for us to live (John 10:10). Honest, persistent, private, and shared prayer is a reliable pathway to God. Here, God is the Person of Jesus Christ, His Father the Almighty, and Their Holy Spirit, the Advocate. When my brave young daughter disclosed her victimization, it was a sudden, unpremeditated report. She stated that being molested by her father started from her earliest memories and escalated in her teen years into several episodes of sexual assault. These occurrences were sporadic, she said, and whenever they stopped, she thought they had stopped for good, so she never told anyone, always with the false hope that it wouldn't happen again.

Within 24 hours of hearing this disclosure from a third party, I confronted my husband about it. In the same time frame other members of the family came forward with their own reports of sex crimes they said he had committed. Trying to understand how and why I never knew about any of it until now caused a spiritual and psychological war inside me that wanted to destroy not only my sanity but my love and trust in God, myself, and others. It didn't win.

Some Terms

The term *sexual violence* as used here is considered a civil *and* a spiritual crime. In addition to breaking civil law, it's an offense against God and His children. It's sin. Our sexuality is a gift from God Who is pure love. When sexuality is dominated by a will to exert personal power over someone else at the expense of his or her inherent dignity, it can no longer be associated with love. It is, as Dante describes all sin, a form of anti-love. There's nothing sexual about sexual violence. It's a power play from an unstable mind that is deceived about love. The deception substitutes envy and lust for love.

Sexual violence is an umbrella-term for all inappropriate sexual conduct, which ranges from verbal innuendo to violent assault. Yet these behaviors, no matter where they fall on the spectrum, rip apart or violate God's intentions because they harm us. The common phrase "sex abuse" doesn't capture this violent element of all such actions, so I tend not to use it.

This book speaks to all three groups affected by sexual violence: perpetrators, survivors (formerly known as "victims"), and non-offenders: those who are associated with either or both of the two other groups but are not considered by the survivors to be participators in the crimes. Many may not be familiar with the existence of non-offenders, but we complete the picture. Because the group of non-offenders is the largest in number, we can become an integral part of breaking the cycle that enables these crimes.

No one *ever* deserves to be sexually hurt. When we care about someone who harms or is harmed by another, we're harmed too. Non-offenders may include anyone associated with the victim, the perpetrator, or both. Primarily, they are those whom the victim does not consider to be an offender.

Victims, or survivors, as they're now called by social service advocates, are those who are the primary targets of offenders.

An important distinction to make with regard to the offenders addressed in this book has to do with their self-perception. *If they can be accountable for their actions and admit to needing help, they distinguish themselves from those who remain steeped in denial.* Perpetrators who sincerely desire to stop putting themselves and others at risk are in a separate category from those who do not. Convicted sex offenders and those still hidden in our neighborhoods may or may not fall into this category.

Perpetrators are described here as male because the majority of them are, according to the Bureau of Justice Statistics. While I haven't overlooked that women are guilty of sexual crimes, I use male pronouns to describe perpetrators because men comprise the majority in this group.

How, Why, and When This Book Was Written

As of this date our case has not gone to court because of insufficient evidence. Survivors who may have contributed exact dates, places, and further details were unwilling or unable to come forward. The latest survivor said she couldn't remember any information other than her initial statement, which was taken within weeks of the most recent crime against her.

Without hope for a trial, I began to hold court inside myself. Our identity as a family had been completely usurped. In the pain of watching the consequences of the crimes turn my then teenager into a stranger to me and to herself, I could only ask one question: *Where was God in all this?* I knew Him as our Guide and Protector; the Person Who was infinite mercy and love. As I talked to those who worked with perpetrators or had victims in their own families, I kept raising the question, *If God promises to be our help in all things, why are we thinking and talking about sexual violence as though it is the exception?*

This lack of a spiritual perspective on sexual violence raised endless questions for me. If Christ performs miracles, where are they for people like us? Why isn't the Church using her ministries of healing to seek us out and restore us? Can I rely on God to save us from among those going down into the pit (Psalm 130)? Can I say, as a person of faith, that despite suffering this prolonged and multi-faceted agony, "all will be well,"[1] and truly mean it?

Through prayer, I began to experience God's grace as an active force that spoke directly to me. And if He would do that for me, it was reasonable to believe He would for others, too. I understand God as a healer of body, mind, and soul, but when I shared this idea with others who were going through the aftermath of sexual violence it was often thought to be "too heavy" or even convoluted.

Yet it's widely agreed that one person's experience affects a large group of others. An offending priest, for example, injures his victim, the family of the victim, and the congregation as a whole. We feel the victim's pain with and for him or her, but not in the same way as the victim does. The whole situation gets cloudy with loyalties and lies. The scientific perspective is more easily viewed as impartial, and for that reason people feel more comfortable using its language and listening to it as an authority. The spiritual aspect of the human being is often trampled, or confused in the public sphere with a *religious* response. Religion holds out beliefs, practices, and traditions specific to it, while spirituality is part of all of us, an indelible, irrevocable part.

This distinction shouldn't cause upset while you read these pages. Our souls are the immortal part of our human nature, integrated and inseparable from it. Because I'm Catholic, my understanding of God and the spiritual life is enhanced by the *Catechism of the Catholic Church* (CCC), which is scripture-based, but we are a universal Body searching for God's will and the intimacy that comes from following it, as many others do. The Biblical references here are from *The New American Bible*.

You'll see italic type used throughout the text. My conversations with others as I researched often had an impact on me that was like encountering a meaningful poem or a poignant sound bite. Using italics helped me underscore the often chaotic and surreal experience of sexual violence as well as the courageous struggle of those searching for new life in its wake.

The story I tell here for the glory of God is meant to witness to the truth that our crosses, of every size and kind, have a profound and unifying factor. They are designed for victory. After all, Christ died upon His own cross and was raised up again. His victory over death has secured for us forgiveness for our every wrong deed. When someone pays our way, if we respond with deep gratitude it can change us. Spiritually, that change brings about a conversion. Part of our conversion is seeing our wrongs and deciding to repent for them. When we repent and receive God's forgiveness, it helps us commit to a new way of life. One that has more love for the Lord in it. These actions in the soul are the result of responding to grace. Grace has one purpose, to accelerate our growth in holiness.

Non-offenders and survivors may argue that they have nothing to be forgiven for. I know I did. But forgiveness is a vast territory. More than a place, it is a force for inner freedom made of a protective peace—peace offered by the very hand of God. All it takes is acceptance of the gift *and* the Giver. As non-offenders, strong in number, we can become strong in the truth we carry. We are hurt by this crime, and we want the hurt to stop so we can let God truly and deeply heal us, all of us.

My foundational message as a non-offender is the same as the universal cry of the heart when it finds God's care in the middle of trial. The message is clearly one that saves: *We are not alone.* God *was* there in our experience. God *is* there in our memory. God *will always be* with us.

If we allow God in, if we let our story include God, Who is our Father, His Son, and the Holy Spirit, we won't be crushed under the weight of the cross. Little by little we'll see how we are cherished by the God Who made us for His loving, life-giving embrace. We will learn about Him and about ourselves as we are healed and brought to the truth. And the truth is this: We are God's beloved children. You either want that identity or you don't. If you do, but don't know if you can live it, He'll show you how. He'll meet you in your heart and bring you into His own.

Format

Abusive behavior typically occurs in a cyclical pattern. When I tried to examine the problem of sexual violence in a linear way in order to come to "the end," I found the task impossible. As soon as some aspect seemed understandable, another more confounding would surface.

Then a phone call with a stranger gave me some direction. He was a priest counselor a local pastor referred me to. Before we finished our brief call, he assured me that something *good* would come from my ordeal. I was stunned. Then he said a sentence I'll rely on for the rest of my life. As we confirmed our arrangements to meet, he added, "You've got to trust. *Trust is the ultimate weapon.*"

Praying about the word *trust* during the days that followed, I remembered it was the start of a penitential chant I'd learned years earlier. The entire chant has only four words. These words became four chapter titles: "Trust," "Surrender," "Believe," and "Receive." Each chapter is a mixture of research, lived experience, and revelation based on scripture and prayer. God works in people who allow Him the room. See if you can let each word of the chant reach a place in your soul where God can sit and stay with you a while (Revelations 3:20).

Social science research as well as the Catholic Catechism acknowledges that the grievous harm caused by this sin *scars for life*. We can choose to *heal for a lifetime* instead. Although you may have carried your experience alone for years, finding God's plan for your restoration is not a solo journey. The list of resources at the end of the book may prove helpful here. If you suffer from psychological or substance-abuse problems, it's best to address these first. Dealing with the wounds caused by sexual violence is a full-hearted commitment and calls for us to be open to receive loving, prayerful support. Speaking of prayer, I've found it to be an essential staple in the household of healing. In particular, praying with scripture and receiving from it a daily resolution is an excellent means of spiritual growth and well-being.

The blank pages in the back of the book offer a place to note your thoughts concerning what you've read. At the end of each chapter there are a few questions for reflection that might help you start writing.

Sexual violence is one of the most damaging events we can suffer, but it's never too late to live more fully—even if you're in jail, suicidal, or a longtime addict. God calls us to come to Him in ways we can hear right now. And He will always help us answer this call. Some of us think, *God has nothing to do with this. He never did.* But He does. He has everything to do with it. The fear or indifference that may cling to our hearts can be left behind in the tides of His grace. It's deep inner work to accept God's healing. Good, honest work, like you'd find on a farm for your soul. *"Come and see"* (John 1:39).

Except for referenced resources, most names have been changed to protect the privacy of individuals.

✦

ღ�

Trust

ღჃ

✦

1

P icture a handful of seeds being grabbed by God and flung into fertile soil. The flowers and their fruits spring up instantly at His feet. The seed, scripture tells us, is the Word of God. Through it, we learn of God's infinite mercy and saving grace. Yet grace and mercy are gifts of supply, and supply is designed to meet a need. If we can acknowledge our need for God and His goodness, it will help us stay open to hearing Him and acting on what we hear. The more we do this, the more God's truth comes alive and frees us.

Why should we trust God to step into our experience of sexual violence? Haven't we been through enough? The simple answer is, He alone is completely trustworthy. He's proven Himself. He died for love of us and rose from the dead. He's the source of all love, and love is what heals.

My Story

When news of the clergy abuse scandal broke in the *Boston Globe* in 2002, only one of us at home could see cause and effect at work. It was during the week of the Boston trial for the offender priest, John J. Geoghan.[2] While I was busy with household chores, my husband passed through the room and then stopped with an abrupt question. "Tell me something," he said. "Do you think they should lock that priest up?"

"Absolutely," I answered.

"Really?" He seemed genuinely surprised. "I would have thought that you, being a true believer and all...I would have thought you'd have some compassion for him."

"No," I shrugged. "It's a crime no matter who does it."

"*Reealllly?*" He dragged on the word, trying to give me time to reconsider.

I didn't know it then, but this was a deliberate probe of my loyalties. My husband was beginning to weigh his options. The news about the scandal had hit him right where he lived. He got the message quick. There'd be no sympathy from me.

In August of that year, Geoghan was attacked in prison and died of his injuries.

By the end of that year, my father, whose health had been failing, passed away peacefully at his home. We attended his funeral services at my parents' parish in a small town at the Jersey Shore. My husband and daughter returned to our home in New England the day of the burial, and I stayed an extra day at Mom's with two of my brothers.

When I got back home, the atmosphere in the house was quiet—too quiet, somehow. At first I reasoned that it was just an aura of natural sadness. We had just buried a loved one, and it was Christmastime with a lot to reflect on. But by January, the quiet turned to tension. My daughter, then 15, was running out late at night. She met with friends, and then returned to the house very early before we were awake. She was angry and rebellious, often yelling at both of us. I knew she was having a hard time with life in general; her father had been a troubled drinker all her life. But why was she so angry now? And what was going on with her late-night disappearances? I went to the local police about it, because I sensed she was in more trouble than we knew, and it was beginning to scare me.

Al-Anon 12-step meetings were a regular event on my schedule by that point, and recently my daughter had been to the program for teens a few times. Living with the alcoholism of loved ones for almost 30 years, I began to suspect our family dynamics were in for a major change. On a good day my attitude about this pending change would be fairly detached. The 12 Steps and my faith were tools that had always helped me cope. I was sure that when my daughter decided to pick them up for herself, she'd get help too, but now she seemed to be in a place of breakdown. She didn't want to listen or comply with anything.

On an afternoon during the third week in January, I was folding laundry in the basement and felt a distinct presence there that was not good. When I tried to identify the feeling, the word *treachery* came to mind. Standing in front of the wooden drying rack that was next to the oil burner, I tried to analyze the situation further. Since we had recently buried my father, I thought perhaps this was grief, but grief has nothing to do with treachery. *Treachery* was such an odd word to come up with; it made me think of stories about pirates or murderers, but it fit somehow. It felt like there was something powerful in that basement, something hidden and waiting to spring. My instant reflex was a repeated order that said, *"Pray against It."* Right there, in front of the drying rack I started. *Lord, you're going to have to put whatever it is right in front of me. And please, give me the strength to bear it.*

For three days afterward I repeated the invocation to Saint Michael the Archangel. Then it happened. The news came in a phone call from two states away. The caller was Fr. Jay, a Franciscan priest and spiritual leader of the youth group my daughter belonged to. He knew the trouble my daughter was having lately and had arranged for her to spend the weekend with a family we knew whose cabin was up the hill from his friary. It was through these friends that Fr. Jay first sent word for me to be somewhere in the house where I wouldn't be overheard when he called. Then my dread took solid form.

Fr. Jay told me that the night before, my daughter had disclosed to him and the couple she was staying with that her father had sexually abused her for years. The crimes were intermittent but on-going from her very first memories. I never knew and never suspected it. This was treachery all right, the ultimate betrayal and deceit. Finding out kicked my heart out and left me aching for death.

As with any report, there's the message and then there's the messenger. For all the terror in hearing about the violence, in time I thanked God for the way He chose to tell me. Because the messenger was a holy priest, I never had to argue with or accuse anyone to get at the truth. But because it was a holy priest, I couldn't deny it either.

I had no idea what to do with what I had heard, but God knew, and He spoke it straight through His priest. When Fr. Jay said she had been assaulted, I dropped the phone. He repeatedly called my name until I picked it up again. Then I heard myself say, *"Do you think she might be lying? She's been lying a lot."* It was a plea for mercy.

"No...I'm sorry. I'm sorry I had to tell you like this. I wish I could be there with you." I didn't realize it then, but his emphatic "no" was a tremendous gift. Because of it I never doubted her, not once, no matter how much she tried to make me.

The blood started to leave my brain. I could hardly push out the words. *"What do I do?"*

His voice was quick and clear. *"Go to the police."*

"Oh. Yeah. Okay."

It was as though I was hypnotized and had just gotten a command from the magician. For years afterward I replayed that four-minute memory, especially when reading accounts of non-offenders who are condemned for not doing anything to stop the predator or for deliberately covering up the crimes. I might have acted exactly the same if it hadn't been for Fr. Jay. Because I trusted that he loved God and cared about us, I could trust he was telling the truth. Even though I was sickened with fear by what he told me, I felt empowered to do the right thing and report it.

Even though it was easy for me to say to my husband that every offender deserves to be arrested, until you're in the moment you don't know how your beliefs are going to play out. It reminds me of the feeling I got from William Carlos Williams's poem "The Red Wheelbarrow." He says *"so much depends upon"* it. So much depends on what we do in the moment, with the truth, and the power of disclosure.

When I discussed this issue with a priest years later, he admitted that when reports first came out to pastors or bishops, the best response they could come up with (which often wasn't chosen) was to put the offender into psychiatric care and then eventually return him to active duty. It was believed during the 1970s that counseling could cure. Now we know otherwise. Part of the reason someone doesn't receive effective treatment (for those offenders who want it to succeed) is not a lack only of accountability but also of wisdom. When there's trouble in the house you must go outside of its bounds for help. More on that later.

After the terrifying phone call from Fr. Jay, I needed to get out of the house quick. I packed a few things in a knapsack and told my husband I'd be at the university doing research. Since it was my last semester in graduate school, going to the library on Sunday afternoons was fairly routine. The local police station was a 10-minute drive from our house in the same direction. It was near suppertime, and the lobby was empty when I arrived. The woman behind the sliding glass window said the juvenile detective had someone in his office but she'd tell him I was waiting.

I had met with the detective once or twice before because of my daughter's truancy. He went to our church and was a mild-mannered guy who seemed fatigued with the pressures of his job—although you could tell he wouldn't trade it for another.

It wasn't long before he greeted me and we walked to his small, sparsely furnished office. His face was expectant. I still couldn't believe what I had to tell him. It was a short report. Then he fired his questions. *"Where's your husband now? Does he know that you know? How much did you tell him?"*

My answers fired back on automatic. Watching him listen to me, an eerie thought flashed through my mind. *He's not surprised about this.* I asked him if he had already known about my daughter's abuse. His reply landed another swift kick. *"When you're running away, you're running* from *something. This is usually what it is."*

There's nothing like flat facts. In connection with sexual violence, here's my number-one finding: There are those who know about it, and those who don't. What you don't know can definitely hurt you. Then I asked the detective the same question with the same sinking feeling I had had on the phone with

Fr. Jay. *What do I do?* My blank mind and heart made me a stranger to myself in the last half hour. The detective gave me a phone number for the rape crisis hotline, saying, *"They'll help you. Just tell them what you told me. And come in tomorrow with your daughter so she can make a statement."*

This was procedure. This was routine. This was my family dropping into a bottomless pit. The telling-of-it had begun. My conversation with the hotline counselor was swift but strengthening. *"Tell her you believe her. Tell her you'll get her help."* Simple and straight, I could do that. What I didn't know was that no one else involved would feel the same.

During the days that followed, in meetings with drug-abuse counselors, priests, lawyers, psychologists, and 12-step program members, I repeatedly found myself the only one in shock over my situation. Up until then I hadn't had a clue that sexual violence is a common outcome among troubled family members, especially substance-abusers who don't get help. *Why didn't I know?*

That question took on a life of its own and followed me everywhere I went, for years. Within 24 hours, both the offender and my daughter denied the crimes had ever happened. I drove overnight to pick her up at the couple's cabin, and I called her father from there. I told him I had made a report to the local police and commanded him to do the same. *"Go to the police and tell them the truth,"* I barked at him. *"They already know it anyway."* His answer was a black yell. He denied it all, calling our daughter a liar.

Then I changed tactics and pleaded. *"She has her whole life ahead of her,"* I screamed into the phone. *"You* have *to tell the truth! You* have *to—for her sake!"* This was sheer panic, no tears yet.

27

"NO! NO! NO!" he roared. I hung up.

It was 6:30 in the morning the day after the disclosure. It would be years before we spoke again. I realized his denial was the manic response of a base, animal fear. It terrified him. It made him turn on his own and shoot to kill. When we got back home that afternoon, my husband's car wasn't in the driveway. Good. We could get a few things we'd need while we were staying away.

Suddenly the phone rang. I hesitated, but then said hello. It was Nyla, a family member from up north. She had heard what was going on with us. She said it wasn't the first time he had done this. *"He molested both my girls,"* she said in one gulp. There was nothing left for me to breathe. "Why wasn't anything *done* about it?" I screamed back. *"Why didn't anyone ever tell me?"* At this point I pulled my daughter over to the phone so she could hear every word.

"We thought you knew," Nyla said. "Remember when Katelyn told her teacher about him?"

In a flash of memory I saw a phone call my husband received more than 15 years ago. It was from his mother. They had a vehement exchange that ended with his telling me his family was all crazy, and *"Don't ever believe anything they tell you."* The story went that his niece had made a report to one of her teachers about her uncle's unwanted touching. His mother heard about it from Nyla, and then called my husband. The outcome amounted to a verbal slap on the wrist. He denied all wrongdoing and then stayed away from everyone at holiday-time for a few years. That was it.

"Talk to Kristen," Nyla insisted on the phone now. "She'll tell you. She just found out what happened. Go over there."

Realizing what my husband had done horrified me, but at the same time it felt like a strange blessing. This meant my daughter and I weren't alone. We could all stand in the truth together.

"We're going to Kristen's," I announced. *"She'll go with us to the police."* The next stop was over the bridge, and we had to move fast. He could already be headed back home. When we arrived at Kristen's, my daughter stayed in the car. She seemed to be calculating something. I walked up to the second floor to the main entrance of Kristen's apartment and called her name, telling her why I'd come. She tried to stall me, saying that she hadn't told her own family what had happened yet. *"We've got to talk about this. Let's sit down,"* she said, as she moved toward the kitchen table.

"Talk? She was raped!" I was frantic.

What was blocking Kristen from seeing how desperate this was? "You've got to help me! She fought with me all the way down here from up north this morning. She's wild and she needs help. She's so angry! It's so awful!" I couldn't bear to hear another no. I was sure my daughter's life, all our lives, depended on staying together in this.

Kristen suddenly agreed, saying she'd quickly change and get in the car with us. Shortly after we got to the police station, as my daughter made her statement in another room, two detectives came in and asked Kristen if she would answer a few questions. They left me alone for about 15 minutes. During that time Kristen reported that my husband had abused her when she was a young girl. It had started when she was nine. The police weren't involved, Kristen said, and my husband never went for any professional help. But today, so many years later, God was giving this loving middle-aged woman the courage to tell her story, and the grace to be believed and respected for it. God brings light out of darkness.

For the next few days I stayed with a friend in town while my daughter stayed with friends elsewhere. She wanted nothing to do with me. Whenever I looked at her now all I could think about was how much she must have suffered all those years. It nearly broke me completely. It caused a deep alienation between us that was really a reflection of the estrangement we felt from ourselves. All I could do was begin to let the story breathe on its own by telling those who loved us. It was a wounding story, but I had incredibly strong friends who were my family in faith. They could listen and not turn away.

It was just before sunset when I arrived at Donna's cottage. We couldn't talk alone at her house — the kids were around — so we got in my car and drove down the street, turning into the sandy entrance to the beach. Looking over at my friend, I sensed her patient attention. It gave me courage.

The feeling reminded me of how easily our friendship had started back when our kids were in grade school. Since then we'd shared more than a few troubled times, but we'd also built a trust in God together. No matter what the current crisis, it always seemed that with time and prayer, whatever was happening would be resolved.

Locking my eyes on the empty ocean in front of us, I watched its gray mounds roll against the darkening sky above it. The sky and water together seemed to make a huge, impenetrable wall. My heart was heavy and afraid. *I'm so ashamed to tell her*, I thought. Then, using the momentum of the breaking surf for confidence, I let the words rush out. They were the same words Fr. Jay used. *I'm sorry to hurt you by telling you this…*

Donna watched me intently until I had finished. Then she leaned over and put her arms around my shoulders. The gesture let my sobs loose. She stared at the dimming sea and said slowly, *"Look out there. See those birds? How they rise with the waves and then they're covered over when it breaks on them? They come right back up again. That's what you'll do, my friend."* I found the birds through blurry vision. *"They are there because it's their time to be there,"* she continued. *"Just as you are where you are. They find what they need and then go on. So will you."* Her composure was worth even more than her beautiful words. Was this what healing would be like?

The next day meant going to family court to get a restraining order, and the procedure almost got tripped up. While waiting for our case to be called in the large crowded lobby outside the various court rooms, I briefly separated from the advocate assigned to accompany me, as my husband's lawyer approached. I remembered he had drawn up our will a few years earlier, but he reintroduced himself anyway and said he was representing my husband.

Looking steadily at me, he asked, *"Do you intend to file for divorce?"* His tone was almost inviting. I hesitated for a second, taking in his dyed brown hair. Suddenly I blurted out, "That's not on the agenda right now. Something else is."

Then it was his turn to hesitate before he nodded, turned on his heel, and disappeared. Answering as I did surprised even me. I learned later that if I had said yes to his question about divorce, it would have entitled him to motion to the judge that the restraining order be deferred pending the settlement of visitation rights. Besides obtaining the court order that day, my refusal to divorce gave me time. It would take a lot time to learn how to be true to myself again.

In the end, disclosure causes division when the truth gets lost. The local district attorney in my county said she saw it often: *"I've seen families torn completely apart by disclosures of sexual abuse. There are loyalties, fears, and lies involved. It's so sad."* Yet even in the middle of the devastation caused by the truth coming out in our family, the Lord was fashioning a new life for me to live. The words of St. Paul that my friend Joel spoke to me before we moved away were already coming to fruit: *"Where sin increased great grace abounded"* (Romans 5:20).

Joel wanted to comfort me sharing those words on the phone as I sat crouched in my chair holding my head in one hand. They were God's promise to remain faithful to us. He doesn't abandon anyone to the evils of sin but instead grants us the inner strength to follow Him through darkness and sorrow. I clung to the sense of direction in Joel's calming voice. He was a deacon at our local parish with four children of his own, the youngest only a year older than my daughter. *"I will pray for her,"* he promised me. *"And for you. And him,"* he said, meaning my husband. *"I'll pray he reaches for forgiveness, because that's what we must do. Forgive."* The seed was planted.

I knew Joel was right, but forgiveness seemed useless. My reasoning was shattered into thousands of questions I had no answers for. *What good would forgiveness do? It wouldn't change anything.* But the hope of forgiveness had been planted in me and eventually it would illuminate my mind. Even though I was unaware at the time, from the instant the disclosure broke, God's mercy swept in alongside it. That mercy kept my heart open to His invincible love, a love that even the darkest sin cannot lessen or change.

Not realizing sexual crimes carry a spiritual impact can give them the power to dominate and define whomever they touch.

This is how these crimes and their resulting traumas become the focal point of therapy sessions and court cases. I was certainly headed in that direction, but God's mercy saw to it that I didn't stop asking Him what He would do for us so I could get His answer sure and true. *Save us from our enemies,* His Spirit seemed to breathe in me. That's what God would do. Whoever and wherever they were, outside or in.

People who remain victims of unresolved trauma end up being unable to trust or relate to others. How do we break free from such a chokehold? The insidious self-hatred I felt because I hadn't known about or suspected the crimes would destroy me if I couldn't stop it. My waking hours, so full of taunting thoughts about being duped, soon became obsessed with doubt about everything, including my daughter's love for me. This created a despair I felt no one could understand or free me from, except God. But what was taking Him so long? Hadn't I tried to be faithful to Him? Was I deceived in thinking that too? I had to trust He had His own way and His own time, and whatever His plan, it would be good.

Disclosure and Denial: The One-Two Punch

"Those who trust in him shall understand truth..." (Wisdom 3:9).

When disclosure of sexual violence happens, denial isn't far away. Usually, it's a package deal. The reason is summed up in one word: fear. Not just any fear, but incredibly strong, strangling fear. Between what *usually* happens with disclosure and what *can* happen with God's grace is a chasm between Heaven and Hell. Rock solid as denial can be, God's will is to break through it. After all, Jesus *is* Truth (John 14:6).

The chaos that ensues after the clash of truth with the kind of lying involved in sex crimes is so potent it often gives the sense of time stopping. That's because eternal forces are at work. Eternity can be a valuable concept if your experience of the crime happened decades ago. In that eternity is our God, Eternal Life (John 17:3). This means God is always in the now. So what happened to you, or because of you, is right in front of Him, right now. With trust in Him, you can face your past at any time; in fact, as far as God's concerned, the sooner the better.

One meaning of the word *denial* is rejection. Denial of a truthful report of sexual violence, whether that denial takes the form of minimizing, blame, outright lying, or disbelief, is all aimed at one target: an uncomfortable or frightening truth. Disclosure and denial of a sex crime are a perfect fit. Rejection of something (or someone) is an exercise of personal power, and this is the main diet of sexual violence. No matter what our motives, denial offers us a place to hide inside our heads. Unfortunately, the longer we stay, the higher the rent.

Disclosure is the first battle cry in what can become a very long war when denial is involved. Denial wants to change our minds about the truth. But what it really does is make clear two possible choices: either hold on to the truth you know is true or face your cowardice in all your denials. I was terrorized when our offender refused to admit his guilt even though he knew it would further damage our child. Yet his reaction is typical. He had no qualms about stonewalling. He had a history.

Currently in the media is the revelation of widespread sexual violence in the Catholic Church with all the swollen wounds surrounding who knew what and when. As important as those questions are, I think there's another with greater impact. Did the people who knew about the crimes know *what to do to stop them?* I didn't. I had to be told by someone else. Over and over again. I knew the crimes were wrong but *the shock made me believe I didn't know what to do.* A direction had to come from *outside the circle* of involvement. It's one thing to make a plan that from now on there'll be Zero Tolerance of sex crimes, resulting in full accountability. But it's another thing when someone you've known and likely cared about or even admired for years as one persona suddenly becomes the Enemy. It frightens and disturbs you to your core. This isn't my offer of excuse for those who don't report. It's my experience from having reported. When you're in charge and the buck stops with you, there must be protocol and personnel anchored *outside* the house to answer to.

Why? What makes this so important? Involvement from the outside is how the secrecy can be broken down. When people are scared, they often hide. This was probably why the detective asked if our offender knew that I'd found out about the crimes. He wanted to gauge his reactions. The patterns of offenders are classic, but if you don't believe the crimes happened, if you *can't believe* because you don't know what to do about them, then doing nothing feels like the right response.

Rev. Bill Anderson, a Baptist pastor in the Midwest, experienced a situation of stonewalling that is detailed in his book *When Child Abuse Comes to Church.*[3] In it, we learn about Donald, who was twelve years old when a parent in Anderson's parish reported that he suspected the boy of abusing his child. Confronting Donald initiated an intense battle of wills to see who would stay in control—the offender or the pastor, who was expected to protect others from him.

Denial and all its dynamics are built to last. Everyone in the parish seemed to experience some effect of it over time. There were parents who didn't want to accept the truth that their children had suffered at the hands of this boy, and there were parishioners who sided with the offender and ended up leaving the congregation in order to show their support. Anderson worked tirelessly with police and counselors, guiding all involved toward the truth of what had happened and a path of healing. Round after round of questioning, praying together, and assembling for informational meetings with the parish at large contributed to an eventual conviction that took almost two years. In the end Donald was found guilty of sexual crimes against 60 children.

Instead of letting the negativity implode his position, Anderson tackled the problem with tenacity and prayer. He understood the threat against the goodness of his parish embodied in the violence and deceit. He stood firm in the truth that God would not desert him or his people. As a non-offender, who loved survivor and perpetrator alike, he assumed authority over the dilemma and brought the truth out into the open.

Most of us aren't aware that an adolescent sex offender can be just as vicious as an adult, inflicting beatings, rape, and threats of murder. What we don't know can often cause the most shock, and shock fuels our disbelief. Lies and disbelief, says Anderson, are the twin blades of denial's sword. The young offender's denial held up the due process of law as well as his court-mandated therapy. But thanks to Anderson's faith and the wisdom it afforded him, Donald now has a chance to make vital life-decisions in his adult years with honesty and support.

Disclosure: How It Happens, *If* It Happens

Plenty of unseen, unspoken agony usually comes before a disclosure, so much so that the victim will often deny what he or she has revealed just to get relief from the shock of having let it out. Diana, a student at the community college where I was teaching, sent me a few emails describing how she had disclosed her own experiences years earlier. It seemed she was still working through the pain of breaking her silence. She writes:

> The first time I told anyone was when I was 16 during a therapy session. I was put in counseling by my parents then because of my anorexia, etc. [I]t was spontaneous because I didn't plan 2 mention it…just kinda happened that way. Although the counselor was nice, I felt embarrassed and abandoned…as if something was wrong w/ me for talking about it or trying to. Even now, it's much easier for me 2 write things like that in a journal than ever verbalizing them. @ first it seemed as if telling some1 was the worst mistake I'd ever made.

Disclosure is dangerous. The only situation more dangerous is not disclosing. According to the Rape, Abuse and Incest National Network (RAINN) in Washington, D.C., 60 percent of sexual assaults are not reported to police, and 97 percent of all rapists will never spend a day in jail. However, if you are on the side of truth, God will be with you. If you turn to Him, He will not fail to lead you to safety.

Disclosure, when it's honest, is an example of grace in action. Although it often collapses when those involved retreat into silence, we're slowly learning that when we pursue goodness for its own sake, an imperishable fruit is gained. We come to recognize, as I didn't in the beginning, that evil is an intelligent force that stops at nothing in order to devour its prey, and yet it can be stopped. In sexual crimes the first line of defense is a successful disclosure. So let's look at what makes the measure of success.

Successful disclosures bring about an action of grace that cuts the victim free and stops the violence. A successful disclosure sets off a chain reaction of safe and responsible choices that aid the victim and hold the perpetrator accountable. The best of the successful ones also utilize support from non-offenders. Completely successful disclosures are still not frequent, but they start with reporting, and in particular environments such as college campuses, reporting is on the rise.

Reports of sex crimes are sabotaged most often when the information is shared with someone who can't or won't respond in a responsible and compassionate manner. As we saw in Diana's case above, reporting can result in a variety of negative reactions, often including renewed intimidation from the offender and emotional breakdown in the victim. Once it enters a relationship, the *spirit of Chaos* wants to rule.

When disclosures of sex crimes come from inside institutions, the same panic and shame that individuals experience are played out in the larger group. But where there's a consensus in favor of facing the crime for what it is, positive outcomes can prevail. The following example is of a disclosure that broke open to a larger group, who then voiced their concerns as a community and produced a way to address them that benefitted everyone.

Early in the spring, a neighborhood *kindergarten* in Ocean County, New Jersey, discovered a student had sexually acted out and involved several other classmates.[4] According to the child-advocacy group Stop It Now, at least *one third* of all reported sex crimes are committed by children or adolescents against their peers. As the school board and superintendent handled the situation through appropriate civic channels such as the Division of Youth and Family Services, local police, and the county prosecutor's office, the parents of these five-year-olds clamored for more information. At the time there was no policy in place to notify any parents other than those whose children were directly involved. The superintendent expressed a reaction common to non-offenders in the first stages of dealing with an incident.

"We're devastated by it," he said. *"We're sick over it. This has been our lives for the last two and a half months."* It's no wonder the school wasn't in a hurry to let others in on the details. One parent who attended a school meeting on the subject proposed that the families of the students in the grade involved with the incident should be notified as well as the workers and families involved in the smaller after-care group where the episode took place. Instead of the centuries-old hush-hush attitude, acceptance was bringing out responsible action.

Sexual violence can be stopped by anyone who has facts and courage. A 30-year-old high-school teacher was arrested at his home in Point Pleasant Beach, N.J., and charged with first-degree aggravated sexual assault, endangering the welfare of a minor, and official misconduct after authorities learned of his relationship with a 15-year-old female student. The report was made by one of the victim's friends.[5]

Research has found that when a specific forum to talk about sex crimes is made available, more people, especially children, become willing to contribute what they know. But it happens with adults too. Evidence of this theory was at work in a florist shop in upstate New York.

Kit had a part-time job as a floral arranger in a small rural town there, and for years she had worked with the same group of women. One winter afternoon as the six women sat together at the designing table, Kit began to talk about the sex crime recently reported in the local newspaper. It had happened to a child in the village, and the conversation was about how it had hurt all the people who knew her—not just the primary victim. As she spoke, Kit said, *"There was dead silence in that room. But it turned out that of the six of us, only two didn't know someone personally who had also been involved with an episode."* The silence around the subject was broken because someone, in this case a non-offender, made it acceptable for anyone to talk about it.

Men are finding ways to do much the same when it comes to their own disclosures. We now know more about the differences in how male victims disclose sexually violent episodes in comparison with how females do. This information is empowering victims and those who work or care for them.

Jeff was 19 when he went away to college for the first time. He had excelled in his studies in the past, but with the move to a new environment, his work and attitude slowly began to deteriorate. He became despondent and eventually unable to function, his dad told me. Within a few weeks he returned home and disclosed to his sister that her husband had molested him for years during his early adolescence.

In general, male victims often have more difficulty disclosing to others than females do. In a study designed to examine the perceptions of college students about male victims' disclosure of sex crimes, it was found that the older the victim was at the time the crime was perpetrated, the less masculine and more responsible for the acts he was considered. There are fewer positive reactions connected to males' disclosure to other men, or when the offender was a female.

40

Jeff's disclosure is significant on a number of levels. Not only was he able to truthfully disclose the crimes, but he faced the offender's denial and alerted other family members to the strong possibility that a younger brother had also been harmed by the same man. This disclosure may have seemed unsuccessful on the surface, because his brother wouldn't admit to suffering any abuse, although he showed several physical and emotional symptoms that indicated he did.

Undaunted, Jeff went on to study law with an emphasis on the prosecution of sex offenders, because he was unable to get his offender into court because of a technicality about residency at the time the crimes were committed. The unresolved nature of his past has had another residual effect. His father says that although the two of them never talked about the specifics of his case, there's a lingering impact from it that his son hasn't conquered yet. *"He still lies about some things,"* his father confided. *"It's mostly stupid things that don't really matter, but it's very frustrating."*

For me, one of the strongholds of living my faith is to trust that no matter what we experience in life, God prepares us for it. This belief was sorely tested after our disclosure, but there's no other explanation for my meeting up with Nicole. Shortly after our disclosure, my daughter and I went to a church in the southern part of the state for an afternoon of reflection. It was given by a Franciscan friar from New York City who had done ministry work with our youth group in the past. He had a gift for leading worship with music that he wrote, and there was a good turnout that day.

After the gathering, the crowd exited through the vestibule, and I heard my name called. Looking around, I caught sight of Nicole. Just the week before I had gotten an email from her and all it said was, *"We need to talk. I'll call you."* After reading it, I thought, *She knows something. She knows about us and what happened. But how could she? We haven't seen or talked to each other for over a year.* I remembered how eerie it felt. There was urgency in Nicole's voice as she quickly came up to me and asked, *"How are you? Can we talk?"*

Nicole is a mother of four, articulate, and a quick thinker. She and her husband were very active in ministry at their Catholic parish. The last I'd heard, they had just gotten permission from the bishop to launch a diocesan-wide program for married couples and families. Nicole's third child, a boy named Danny, was only three when we met that afternoon. The oldest was still in grammar school, and the youngest was an infant.

We began to walk across the wide lawn in front of the church as the kids ran around or stood talking to each other nearby. Then Nicole stopped near a tall maple tree. She seemed flustered and yet eager to get something said. She looked me straight in the eye and let it out. *"Just before Christmas,"* she began, *"Danny disclosed that his father has been molesting the three oldest kids."* My heart quit. I stared at her, unable to speak. *"We went to the police,"* she continued, the pain evident on her pretty face. *"Now the state has our case pending in family court. It's been hell."* The air between us became a force-field. Once I told her what happened in my family, we were instant allies.

It takes a lot of trust to disclose sexual abuse and even more to believe disclosing is the right thing to do. Before ours happened, I considered myself to be a fairly trusting person. Afterward, I felt compelled to scrutinize my past family relationships. It was emotionally exhausting. I spent years in an alcoholic marriage and had come to terms with not trusting my husband, but I never imagined his lies and corrupt behavior were harming our child. In my presence he often seemed to be spoiling her.

I realize now that the reason I couldn't see the truth was because I was part of how his charade worked. My subjective impressions, my illusions about who and how he was, all fed into his machine of calculated outcomes. Realizing this was agony on a whole new level for me. When we don't trust someone with whom we have an on-going relationship, this lack of trust imposes restrictions on us. These restrictions can be based on reasonable caution or outright fear. Now I know that although we may not be able to freely say what we think and feel in these compromised relationships, that can't be allowed to inhibit our honesty on any level, especially with ourselves.

Denial in the Raw — Yours, Mine, and Ours

My mother had a saying about human nature that gently excuses our tendency toward denial. She said, *"We can never see ourselves."* Looking at the painful truths connected with sexual crimes when they include the web of denial, what's painful often becomes distorted. Then, not only has the violence happened, but those most closely involved are saying it didn't, or that it doesn't matter that it did. Denial is the backbreaker of trust. Whether it's our own or someone else's denial, it dulls our ability to feel, and feelings help us know what we think and why.

When we're really afraid, denial seems a good idea. It helps us get by — but getting by is a common coffin. Because sexual violence is such a serious crime, if we don't let God into the picture, we run the risk of allowing our *spiritual wounds* to become infected. This will steal the life He has for us, a life of joy. The consequences of severe denial can be physical and psycho–

logical abnormalities ranging from obesity and alcoholism to being accident-prone or suffering intrusive tendencies to harm ourselves or others. These effects aren't limited to female victims but are reported by male survivors, perpetrators, and non-offenders as well. It adds up to a deciding factor. The impact of how we live out our experience of sexual violence is not only long-term but eternal.

For most of us, if we act at all after a disclosure, turning to the justice system for a final solution is the general instinct. But restraining orders are only so potent. They can't keep everything bad away, and they don't prove anything. Shortly after I obtained one for a three-year period, the detective stopped by the house with some news. He wanted to speak with my daughter as well as with me. Then without fanfare he announced the other family members had decided to drop their involvement in the case. My 15-year-old was now his only means of proceeding. Her initial statement didn't secure an arrest warrant because it lacked a sufficient number of details. The attorney general said she needed more dates, times, and places.

"He's calling you a liar, you know," the detective said, baiting my teen's reaction.

She shrugged, staring at the floor in front of her.

"What do you say about that? Are you going to let him get away with it?"

"I can't remember any more," my daughter murmured. My heart sank and sank.

It's important to note here the difference between repression and denial. Sometimes we mix up the two. For instance, we might ask: *How could they not have seen what was happening?* Or, *How can they not remember what happened to them?* We are delicate, sensitive creatures who when deeply frightened begin to fold. One of the folds in your mind is where repression happens. Those who have suffered sexual violence, particularly if it happened before the age of seven, usually have the experience repressed in the subconscious mind. Partial memories may exist, but the individual can't relate the full story, because it isn't accessible.

Our respectful response to the intricate pain of those hurt by sexual violence can help them begin to trust again. But this is easier said than done. Many victims feel they are swimming in foreign waters just living in their own skin. They flirt with symptoms of mental illness that fluctuate by the hour. Post-traumatic stress disorder (PTSD) keeps them under anxiety's thumb. Often they can't control the effects that plague them any better than by popping a pill, starting an argument, or telling a string of white lies. Total denial shifts the pressure to prove what is true and what isn't onto others. All it costs is the effort of repeating the message "no" with an occasional variety of word choice.

We have to *expect* denial to show up in any or all of the persons involved with this crime. If we can, it may help diminish the shock when denial actually happens. After that we must stand firm in what we know is true, no matter what. Our perpetrator's denial wrenched my reasoning loose. I was petrified by it. It proved there was no conscience left in him. The fear this inflicted didn't just put us on different sides of the fence from each other; it meant an entire court case had been squelched. It meant that we had to live with injustice and lies. It meant he had violated all of us once again and gotten away with it.

Or did it?

When we repeatedly refuse to acknowledge the truth about a situation, it's likely denial has *become* our truth. Daily living and relationships must then conform to the dictates of our denial. Eventually, these lies weaken our hope that life can ever be good or safe. Our energies are consumed by the effort it takes to convince others of whatever is needed to float our lies. This was how I assessed the situation after the disclosure occurred and everyone fell silent again. Denial had adapted itself to the new regime. My mother-in-law handed down the decision that there was *"nothing more to say about it."* I had no recourse but to petition heaven. So I did.

One of the first thoughts that came to me was that surely this huge discouragement of losing our legal leg to stand on was one of the reasons Our Lord prayed for us in the garden during His agony. This trial had to be similar to the one He told His apostles about when He said, *"Pray you are not put to the test"* (Mark 14:38).

As I examined what had happened to my trusting nature, questions started to form. Wasn't it my misplaced trust that allowed the violence to happen in the first place? You can't trust untrustworthy people. Trust is earned, not blindly given, and you don't trust someone just because you're related to him. Had I been too preoccupied with my own recovery in Al-Anon or too focused on the issues of active drinking versus sobriety to notice any other troubling behaviors? Alcoholism is a symptom of a deeper ill. The bottom line was, I hadn't known what the broad picture of addiction included.

I took my relationships with my husband and child deeper into prayer with God, my gracious Father. Focusing my thoughts on trusting Him to help me and being guided by scripture fortified my constant fight against confusion and fear. There had been so many lies I hadn't seen. Denial injects a variety of poisons into a situation. One of the deadliest is betrayal. When Peter denied being a follower of Christ, his betrayal was swift: *"I do not know the man"* (Matthew 26:72). The impact of that response reminded me of the round of phone calls I had had with my husband.

Strong fear often defeats love and fidelity. One of the most powerful lies I was tempted to believe was that my love for our family had been a complete failure. After all, the violence had happened while I thought I was doing all I could to love them, working and praying for us to be united, caring, and healthy. This lie, like all the potent ones, had an element of truth to it. It contains a portion of what I believed about love. I *was* doing all I could during those years, but so was God, and He always is. He *never* fails. This disclosure swung open the door to a deep deliverance.

Pope John Paul II told the crowds at a World Youth Day gathering that my daughter attended in Canada, *"There can be no love without truth."* What our disclosure contained was a long-hidden truth. And although it brought separation and death to the family as we knew it, it also brought hope for a new life that only genuine love makes possible. Now each of us knew the truth. What remains is how we'll live it out. The disclosure was God's foot in the door. This is the gift of wisdom from the Lord to anyone who searches for it with hope.

Sex offenders who refuse to admit their guilt suffer lies differently. Their truth has nowhere to go. Like a lie, truth is a force. It's meant for action: to be spread, developed, and taught. Lies are a diversion. They distract with the power of their appeal or their fear-factor. Lies snow us or scare us. Either way, lies are shocking, especially a lie about people or institutions we had thought we knew or loved. Many offenders are driven to deny the truth because they believe their identity depends on it. They build relationships on a specific set of lies so that anything said in opposition can't be true or they lose everything. Their lies make them who they are, to others and themselves. Without someone to believe his lies, the offender becomes nothing, no one. It was explained to me that this is why a convicted criminal will often insist on his innocence. The reasoning he uses is that being a hated person is at least being someone, and he might as well be hated for a lie about his innocence than for a despicable truth about what he did.

Those who perpetrate a sexually violent crime have a story about why they did it that most of us don't want to hear. It's easier to hate and condemn them. Julie Salkeld, a psychologist at an involuntary civil commitment facility for sex offenders in Avenel, New Jersey, works with men she classifies as "the worst of the worst." Approximately 80% have a history of substance abuse. Of the 150 men in each of the two buildings, Salkeld says, "Only a small portion of them don't want to do it again." Their main goal is to see if they can "present well enough to be let out." But some have decided they're not going anywhere, "either because they've burnt their bridges behind them and have little outside support or because they're unwilling to admit the truth about their offense."

Perpetrators use *"weak victims and strong covers,"* says Eugene DeRobertis, a psychology professor at Brookdale Community College in Lincroft, New Jersey. These victims are often young, trusting children in at-risk families such as those harboring active substance abusers, and the undiagnosed or untreated mentally ill. Children who participate in under-supervised faith communities are the classic weak-victim/strong-cover example, but weak victims may also be found among adults with poor self-esteem such as those classified as co-dependent partners of addicts. Often these adults are children from any of the previously mentioned groups who have grown up without encountering sufficiently nurturing role models.

Strong institutions, on the other hand, are an excellent cover for sex offenders because if the offenders are suspected or found out, the reputation at stake isn't just personal; it's public. This makes an accusation bigger than the suspected individual, more dangerous to the one pointing the finger. So membership in a strong institution such as Penn State University or the Catholic Church enables the offender to deftly spin his false image through his job description. This is how some marriages, professions, and civic groups can offer them a safe and acceptable identity. The rest is opportunity. If they see it, they take it.

The perpetrator gets us to buy into his lies because he lives them. Once he can convince someone else that he is who he says he is (a loving father or holy priest or compassionate doctor), there's a mutual agreement. That's his oxygen. And he will do whatever it takes to keep it pumping. It's almost as if the victim doesn't figure into the equation, making the ruse a personal game of intrigue. After all, if the man you're on a "hot date" with looks and sounds good, he *is* good. Isn't he? Once we consent, or even seem to consent to that idea, power is exchanged.

Research shows human beings want to believe the best about each other. It's happier and easier that way. I believed my husband loved our daughter and would never harm her, and yet I saw his alcoholism harm everyone who knew him. Lesson learned: never believe only half the truth is true.

We want to believe the offender is trustworthy when we don't know the truth about him, and we want to condemn him when the truth is brought to light. So where does God stand?

I stumble while trying to live His teachings, but I know one thing about Him: Christ never confuses. At this point He just wanted me to know He was with me, patiently listening. As my prayer became less hysterical and demanding, I was able to begin listening to Him too. Regardless of the offender's denial and betrayal, despite the family's secrecy, God remains faithful to His people. Paul's letter to Timothy assures us that God's faithfulness is deeply connected to His mercy. Paul writes: "If we are unfaithful, he remains faithful, for he cannot deny himself" (2 Timothy 2:13).

As frightened as I was by what the perpetrator did, I was equally horrified by the eternal damnation he'd face if he didn't repent. All of that was in God's hands. My task was staying open to receive the mercy God guarantees to each of us. Mercy seemed beyond my reach, beyond my imagination. And it was. Yet it was all around me. God's mercy was continually flowing through the compassionate people put in my life, the safe shelter I was freely given when we moved away, and the daily access to Communion through which His infinite love flowed whenever I lifted my heart to meet it.

We learn to trust by trusting. Those of us affected by sexual violence may believe we can never trust anyone or anything again. We may even have told ourselves it's a form of personal strength not to trust. It isn't. Distrust feeds a *spirit of Suspicion*. Yet we justify ourselves. *I won't be anyone's fool*, we say, forgetting that without trust we won't have hope. We need to trust those we deem trustworthy.

Prior to our disclosure I believed God is the only Person Who is completely trustworthy, but afterwards I felt I didn't know God at all. How could He love me and let me be so deeply deceived? Prayer tempered that resentment. God probably tried showing me the truth often, but *until I was ready*, I couldn't see it. Remember the prayer request I made in the basement? *Put it right in front of me, Lord, and give me the strength to bear it.* I was finally giving Him my consent to face what He wanted me to face. Then His Holy Spirit acted in power almost immediately.

A large chunk of the truth I needed to own was being the wife of an alcoholic and realizing that addicts often abuse others in addition to themselves. Also, consistent exposure to lies about our own goodness or the goodness of life in general from a source having authority can seriously corrupt our thinking. That's why the truth in scripture is indestructible. *"You are a temple of the Holy Spirit,"* Paul writes to the Corinthians (1 Corinthians 6:19). This truth has a Source that doesn't surrender to attack. What does it tell us about who we are? It says we're a place where God wants to dwell, and this destines us to be holy. When we are strong enough to live the truth, it breaks denial. It brings new life.

Elisabeth

Elisabeth Fritzl was a teenager when her father imprisoned and repeatedly raped her in a sealed apartment beneath their main residence in suburban Austria. She remained there 24 years, bearing him seven children. One of these died in infancy. Her chance for escape came when one of the children was seriously ill and Elisabeth begged for permission to bring her to the hospital. Once there, emergency personnel became suspicious of abuse and notified the police. Both parents were taken into custody and questioned while the hospitalized teen recovered.

When the media broke Elisabeth's story, her father had been arrested and she had been admitted for psychiatric evaluation and treatment. In the months that followed, Josef Fritzl denied the charges of causing the death of his newborn son by neglect and enslavement. The courts prepared to put the 74-year-old in prison for life, but before that happened, God intervened.

In an 11-hour video-taped statement, Elisabeth, with her head slightly bowed, testified in a slow and steady voice, without condemnation, the details of what she and her children had suffered during their long captivity. The evidence was graphic and astounding. Josef Fritzl hid his face behind a blue binder during the first two days of the hearing. He reported to the media that he hid because of shame.

On the third day he walked into court without his shield.

It had been a year of pre-trial preparation and intensive psychiatric therapy. Before reading the verdict, the judge asked Fritzl if he had anything say. In a surprising statement Fritzl reversed his former position. He said in a low voice, *"I plead guilty."* He later admitted he hoped his plea reversal would help his victims recover. When asked about the death by neglect of the infant he fathered by his daughter, he said, "I should have gotten help. I'm sorry.⁶

Elisabeth's refusal to vilify her father allowed him to drop his defenses and hear the truth of her statements in his heart. Denial is distorted thinking that adheres to an individual's perception of reality, but it is not impenetrable. Today, Elisabeth has her own house, which she shares with her children who lived in the cellar as well as the three who were taken upstairs to live in freedom in her father's upper house. They are finally a united family. She's even been able to renew her relationship with her mother, who lived in the main house all the years Elisabeth was imprisoned. Her willingness to remain open to trusting others must draw on a tremendous strength.

The psychologist Erik Erikson defined nine levels of human development and believed that the challenges of daily life could be described as various crises. Most of us are familiar with his fifth stage called the "identity crisis." If our various life trials have negative results, Erikson believed, we adopt negative character traits, while success strengthens the ego with positive virtues. The first stage is the crisis between trust and mistrust. If this crisis is met successfully, the resulting virtue gained is hope. However, if we fail at age two to become trusting of others or ourselves, we'll have other opportunities to reverse that failure.

Erikson is careful to point out that every stage is repeated throughout our lives. The positive or negative status of any particular stage is always subject to change. So let's say right now we decide we want to grow stronger in trust. God will honor that intention. He's on our side.

Several months following Fritzl's sentencing, reports said his daughter Elisabeth had hope now. Maybe it was the first time in her life. Maybe it's forever.

Trust vs. Trauma

Out-patient counselors who were seeing my teenager for her substance abuse told me her disclosure put her beyond their level of care. Now she needed residential treatment. Our only immediate resource was the rape crisis center in the city, and in hindsight that might have been sufficient. I didn't know for certain what to do and no one could tell me. These were times when you wanted to rely on professionals because you had no personal experience to guide you. What I know now is that trauma attacks your common sense. Find a sounding board and then trust you'll be guided to do the next right thing.

My relationship with my daughter was more strained than ever at this point, and having to wait several weeks for an opening at the residence didn't help. One night she left the house late and returned the next day with a burn of unknown origin on the top of her hand.

Within the week my mother came up from New Jersey, and together with a friend, we took my daughter to the state psychiatric hospital for observation. They kept her for ten days. When she was admitted, I was interviewed by a social worker from the Department of Children, Youth and Families. What I remember about that encounter was one of the questions she asked me while filling out her forms.

"What color are your daughter's eyes?" she asked very casually. I told her and then commented how odd I thought it was for her to ask. She said giving the wrong answer is a tell-tale sign of neglect. I later learned some experts believe the impact of child neglect is even more severe than that of sexual violence. That was when I knew this was the strangest world I ever could have imagined, and I wanted out with every fiber of my being.

Our first visit during her stay at the hospital took place in the same room as the interview, a small annex off the main gathering space. It had a steel door with the top half made of safety glass. That meeting was the first and last time I remember her honestly expressing what she felt about what had happened. Coming into the room, she seemed quiet and fragile. We shared the beige Naugahyde sofa across the room from where the caseworker had questioned me earlier. She curled up beside me and began softly crying in my arms. I stroked her thick, long hair, and suddenly she began to shake. *"I'm so sorry! I'm so sorry! I'm so sorry!"* she repeated between sobs. I told her she had nothing to be sorry about and assured her nothing was her fault. Now I think it would have been better if I'd just let her be sad and let it out, but what did I know? I assumed she was focused on the violence, but maybe she was beginning to see how it had overwhelmed the rest of her life, causing the drug use and all that went with it.

The diagnosis was post-traumatic stress. They did not put her on any medications. The treatment options were either a home for abused girls or substance-abuse residential care. Since we didn't have insurance and the home didn't have a reputation for quality care, I decided on the substance-abuse place. Her stay there lasted seven months. The feelings of betrayal and loss were hardly addressed while we were separated. If I wanted to survive this, I had to seek level ground in myself that I could rely on.

Finding Theo

God had made sure that prayer, the sacraments, and spiritual direction were a regular part of my life before I learned about the violence in our family. Then He prepared me for a disclosure of His own—His power to save. The opposition was vicious. Our case of generational domestic violence had continued for so long it seemed to completely discredit who I thought we were as a family and who I was as a member of it. It wasn't long before my emotions snowballed with these thoughts. It felt like my entire identity was in question. I tried reminding myself that feelings aren't facts and that the best I could do was try to see sexual violence for what it is. But the subject wasn't a mere mindset. It was my daughter and the man who called himself my husband. I had thought I was the good mom. Now I was the ultimate fool. I refused to stop praying for help, and help continued to come.

Often this help was the supernatural kind in the form of invisible graces, especially those received from Holy Communion. Sometimes these graces worked through me as inspirations to action. When I first heard the disclosure, I put on a brown scapular and wore it for years. At that time the fear in my mind seemed to threaten to defile my body in some unseen way. Or at least that was the way it felt.

The scapular is a woolen cloth square about two inches by three inches with images of Jesus and Mary on it. The squares are held in place with a ribbon that makes a loop large enough to fit over one's head. It is worn with one square over the chest and the other between the shoulder blades. It shows devotion to the Blessed Mother and disposes the wearer to graces to live a devout life.[7] Wearing the cloth scapular reminded me of my place in God's family. It gave me confidence and courage to keep returning to His house for daily mass and reception of Him in Communion.

After leaving the cathedral in Providence after a daily mass at noon one weekday, I saw a flyer posted on the hallway bulletin board. It said healing prayer would be offered there the following Saturday. My daughter and I frequently attended Charismatic prayer meetings and were comfortable receiving an anointing with blessed oil and individual prayer. That's what I expected at this gathering. It turned out to be an introduction to a specific type of prayer called *Theophostic* prayer. And we didn't just learn about it but were encouraged to experience it first-hand, which most of us did.

Theophostic ministry (now called Transformational Prayer Ministry or TPM) originated when a Christian psychologist named Ed Smith decided he wanted to help his patients beyond the "tolerable recovery" most of them had to settle for. Being a Christian, he knew Christ told His followers that they would do even greater things than He had done. So Ed wanted to cure his chronically ill clients. Video-taped seminars and workbook exercises introduced the concept and practice of Theophostic prayer to us. Smith explained many of his patients, particularly those with a history of sexual abuse, weren't able to claim complete freedom from their post-trauma symptoms even after years of seeing him for help. Yet he knew from scripture that Christ promises His followers authority over unclean spirits. Jesus healed people completely and said we would be able to do the same in the power of His Name. When Smith asked in prayer how this could be possible, the healing Theophostic ministry of prayer was revealed to him.[8]

Theophostic is a word taken from the Greek roots for God (*Theo*) and light (*phostic*) and means "Light of God." According to their website, Theophostic ministry is "a biblically based approach to prayer ministry that leads a person to the feet of Jesus through prayer and allows Him to reveal His truth to the wounded person's heart and mind." TPM is Christ-centered and relies on the power of God for its direction and outcome.

The practice of Theophostic ministry is world-wide today, but according to Smith, it first started with the followers of Christ. He uses the example of the people who lowered their friend through a hole in the roof so Jesus could cure his crippled body. The wounded man *was placed in a position to receive Jesus's help*. Transformational Prayer is the action of Jesus, through His Holy Spirit, speaking truth into our darkness. Each lie we believe, Smith says, causes pain, which continues until the light of God's truth dispels it forever.

The roadblock to healing, Smith explains, is "lie-based pain." This pain is psychologically, physically, or emotionally manifested as negative feelings such as abandonment or rejection. The pain locks us in a lie about ourselves that we are unable to break without the power of the Knower of all truth Who *is* Truth, Jesus.

Smith reasons that just as many of us may discover we unconsciously *tell* lies during the course of our lifetime, it's reasonable to assume we *believe* certain lies told to us as well, especially lies coming from someone who is a strong influence in our life. This explains why people can understand that they're not to blame for being victims of abuse, but their knowing doesn't free them from the pain. The lie we believe is what hurts, Smith maintains, not what actually happened to us; and because the lie is never disproved or resolved, our pain becomes chronic.

Smith doesn't hold that Theophostic ministry is the only way to heal deep spiritual wounds, but he sees it as a complete and lasting way. Learning about Theophostic ministry gave me hope in the power of church ministry to help my family. It showed me how completely God wants to care for their wounds. Learning from people I'd never met before what was happening in the hearts of those I loved put me in awe of God and made me truly grateful despite my daily sense of terror. Being able to share the bond of faith with a community that directly addressed our problem felt like I'd hit pay-dirt. Here was a proven path back into the light of Christ that would free us from the excruciating pain we were living. It never occurred to me that human beings often prefer to reach a settlement agreement with their pain rather than go through it to find freedom. But wasn't it true that I'd often say to myself, "Better the devil you know than the devil you don't"?

The Move

It was close to the seven-month mark of my daughter's stay in rehab when I began hearing the stories from the other parents with girls there. They'd heard about still other girls who went through the same program. *"As soon as they're back on the street, they pick up the drugs again. You gotta really watch 'em."* That threat, along with the possibility of someday dealing with my husband outside of court, put my back against the wall.

My newly widowed mother offered to let us live with her for a while. I loved the idea of being down the street from the Atlantic Ocean at the Jersey Shore, but it meant leaving my own home and friends. Donna helped me decide by looking at the greater good. During the first few years away from home, I often reflected on her simple logic: *When you're hurting, you need love. You go toward the love, not away from it.* The plan was for my daughter to finish the last two years of high school and hopefully make a fresh start.

The night she checked out of the residence, one of the administrators walked us to door and then stood watching as we walked to my car parked down the dark street. Suddenly she called out to our backs: *"The biggest problem will be control. She won't stand anyone having it but her."*

And that's the way it's been.

Within a week we packed what we needed, closed our house, and moved out. Leaving my home of 17 years, I wondered, was I making a leap of faith or just running scared? I didn't know, but God did. He had given me support from friends and my side of the family as well as the promise that Jesus will meet us in prayer to heal this terrible wound. What more could I need?

It was almost Christmas. In fact it was only a few days before the one-year anniversary of my dad's death. That loss was followed five months later by the passing of my second brother, a loved and gifted alcoholic. It was a miracle that my mother, my daughter, and I survived the pressures of our grief—a narrow road indeed. Eventually, all the signs on that road said the same thing. *Stay close to love.* In time I saw there isn't room for anything less than love between us, so that in the dark places of anger and fear, God can plant new growth.

Only weeks out of the residence, my daughter rebelled against having to live with a parent and a grandparent. After a few meetings with an out-patient drug counselor, she refused to contact a sponsor to accompany her to 12-step meetings, so the counselor dropped her case. That made me the watchdog.

"Your recovery is your business," the counselor informed her. "I can't do it for you." I wish I had taken that attitude to heart, but I was more troubled than I knew. By the end of the year she hated her school and hated going to Sunday mass. I took each of her rejections personally, when it was actually a textbook example of the breakdown between family members from an abusive background. All I could see was that the one responsible for the chaos wasn't around to take the blame. It seemed the gates of Hell had moved to my mother's with us.

Yet it was there that my sense of safety slowly returned despite the frequent retaliations of a very angry teenager. She soon decided to shut out her crisis counselor too. Once she stopped her appointments, I started going to my own. Focusing on my trauma instead of my daughter's took time and effort I didn't have at first. Impatient and exhausted, I preferred instead to review countless incidents over the past 15 years that might have tipped me off to my husband's behavior but didn't. In my individual sessions I grilled the kind woman assigned to our case. *"Why didn't I see it?"* I harangued her. *"How could I not have known? What happens in other families that go through this? Are all non-offenders so routinely blindsided?"*

She gave me honest answers that didn't feel like any help. "Every case is different. For every non-offender involved there's a different degree of knowing and not knowing…and you are legion," she said. I was struck by this response from her on a couple of levels. It meant that there were countless numbers of non-offenders all experiencing effects similar to mine. And the word "legion" reminded me of the name of the unclean spirit Jesus cast out from the man who roamed near the tombs (Mark 5:9). There was no shared comfort for me here but instead a sense of camaraderie with the devil himself.

Ironically, it was when my counseling case was closed that my obsession to figure it all out really kicked in. It was as though I needed the freedom to look at my memories alone, without the obligation to tell anyone what I found out that set me off. And a counselor wasn't just anyone. They already knew the bottom line. Why tell them anything? They might figure something out that I didn't or couldn't. The power wrapped around my knowing what happened and not knowing *all* that happened grew stronger in my isolation. Every scrap of it fed my fear.

When I felt myself slipping through the cracks, there was the beach to photograph or journal pages to write. Long walks along the shore in the bright January sun or on the boardwalk until the early moon rose up over the ocean became pictures I eventually found a small market for in town. My heart kept breaking.

Looking for places to pray, I discovered our local chapel kept its doors unlocked until 5:00 p.m. Eventually I saw it was necessary for me to include others, even strangers, in my exile. There were volunteer opportunities at the soup kitchen on Friday nights and the youth group on Sundays. God showed me through these experiences that He is always caring for us, inside and out. Then I was introduced to a woman named Linda Whalen.

An editor and friend of mine from New England asked me if I wanted to review Whalen's book, *Valley of Childhood.* It was a memoir of spiritual healing and insight gained after the experience of childhood sexual abuse. It was providential. In a series of interviews with the author, I learned to see this heinous crime without any legal veils over it. It was sin—serious, deadly, sin—that would keep on hurting us until it was taken to the Lord and settled with Him. Linda didn't claim her healing through sheer will-power. She described it as *"a spiritual battle"* for the life of the soul—one from which she's emerged *"not just a survivor but completely restored and open to all the life God has for me."*

For Linda, the decision to "let go and let God" came gradually. It started during the Catholic Church's era of Renew study and prayer groups in the 1980s. That was when a group near Linda called Women Ministering to Women formed. Sharing scripture and intercessory prayer with this community helped Linda realize she wasn't alone with her pain from the past. She could open her heart and look at the hurt with loving support close at hand. The spiritual path to Linda's healing bore a striking resemblance to the action of grace in Theophostic prayer. This was a tremendous encouragement for me because it held out another path leading to the same destination: God's miraculous healing after the devastation of sexual violence.

It made me hopeful of finding further support for the success of spiritual healing from other sources. It was a watershed moment because up until then the majority of my findings from social scientists, law enforcement, and medical experts confirmed no such thing. For them, the caliber of harm to victims of sex crimes, especially when they were children, was classified in the "scarred for life" category. In my heart I couldn't accept that and still call myself a Christian. Even the uplifting accounts of healing written by victims themselves didn't strike a chord with me. In many of them the narrator was middle-aged and the offender had died before she reached for forgiveness. Our offender was still very much alive, and most of the victims were going through their tumultuous twenties.

Frantic questions continued to gnaw at me. Where did this leave us? Was I just supposed to wait this out? If my family doesn't seek God's help, do I simply stand by and watch them suffer? It was more than I could bear. This was my only child; there had to be something I could do. I railed in prayer. Where was God's compassion and mercy? A soundless reply trickled across my heart in answer. *"God loved the world so much, He gave His only Son"* (John 3:16).

God's ways are not our ways. Once we begin to know them, He wants His life to expand in us. The truth of God's sacrifice silenced me with humble repentance, but not for long.

Oppression

"Guard your heart," the Lord says in the Book of Proverbs, *"for in it are the sources of life"* (Proverbs 4:23). Those of us who have experienced sexual violence may have more difficulty than others when it comes to reflecting on things in our hearts. Trying to keep ahead of the inner anxiety, we may often subconsciously feel ourselves to be in a rush most of the time. But without reflection our conscience becomes dulled. This spreads darkness over our thinking, which can include our thoughts about God, too.

We've all heard people say, *Oh, God has more important things to do than listen to my problems.* That's another version of *God has nothing to do with this.* Once we enter this mindset we can also dismiss our natural entitlement to a life engaged in happy relationships, including the one God wants to share with us. These attitudes are the hallmark of the *spirit of Oppression.*

I was oppressed and didn't know it at first. I didn't admit my own trauma from the violence for a long time. My daughter had suffered so much I couldn't think of myself. It wasn't until I began to really listen to some of my thoughts that I saw my private turmoil. Here's an example of what I mean. Standing in a long line at a checkout in a busy grocery store, I imagined striking up a conversation with the person in front me, just to kill some time. *What would* you *have to say?* I chided myself. My feelings of alienation were often overpowering because I'd recently lost my home.

Everyday reality often felt completely incommunicable. Whenever I tried to picture us getting through this ordeal, I hit a wall. Then icy self-doubt would flood every juncture where I needed to make a decision. *If you didn't know about the crimes, what else can you ever be sure of?* How much I didn't know became an obsession and usually hit me hardest just sitting at a red light. In prayer I begged God to guard my heart. It's the nature of evil and the sin it spawns to keep on destroying unless it is stopped. Then, once it's stopped it must be permanently blocked. In other words, our spirit must be transformed and filled with the Spirit of God in order to keep the evil at bay. The parable of the man who was delivered from an evil spirit in Matthew 12:43-45 shows what happens if you simply try to resume your old habits after being freed.[9] You become even more endangered than you were before.

When our offender denied his crimes but failed a lie detector test, what kept wounding me was his capacity to lie. If he had only admitted the truth, we could work with it. Lies sink everything in a great abyss.

When Nicole was in the final stages of litigation against her husband, he began stalking her and the children. He put sand in her gas tank. He showed up and silently harassed her in public places. He knew she was exhausted with grief and anxious over the safety of her kids, and any way he could contribute to that could only help him. He wanted to plea-bargain. She wanted jail time. The defense lawyer used every angle possible to prolong the trial date. Her husband often broke the restraining order and got away with it.

Unrepentant offenders want to keep us victims. That's domination and tyranny. That's oppression. When I asked Nicole what she would want from her husband if she was able to talk to him, she didn't hesitate. She wanted the truth. She wanted him to admit his wrongdoing to the kids so they could be free of the burden they carried because of his lies.

Weary as I was, the Lord still reached me through scripture. "But I will show you whom you should fear: Fear him who, after your body has been killed, has authority to throw you into hell. Yes, I tell you, fear him" (Luke 12:5). I needed to constantly remind myself that it wasn't the exact details of the crimes that mattered but the effect their wounds had on us. Evil isn't out to maim but to kill, and not just our physical well-being. The Oppressor will try to keep our focus on him and what is about him or on ourselves and what we are suffering; whatever it takes to keep us distracted from God's love and mercy for us. He may use mental anguish, continued forms of abuse, or both. If it confuses, it can ensnare. If evil gets a foothold, we'll go down.

God tells us, *"Wisdom will vindicate her children"* (Luke 7:35), and that means whether the evil-doer complies or not. The grace of wisdom helps us see we don't need validation from the offender in order to be restored. That's another lie. It would feel better if they admitted their guilt and showed remorse, but it's not necessary for our healing. It's necessary for their salvation.

Triggers

Since sexual sins are steeped in secrecy and shame, we inevitably stifle what we know about the subject. But triggers often release a gut reaction in our thoughts or feelings. Triggers mean there's pressure to release. They can be psychological or physiological in origin. A scent in the air or a sudden sound or a type of environment can instantly bring up an image or memory attached to a trauma from the past. When triggers are biologically based, they may be due to the hormonal changes common to menopause, puberty, or pregnancy.

Because our culture is quick to minimize past trauma with the bustle of "moving forward" and "finding closure," we may miss an opportunity to look at our triggers with God and find a doorway that leads to a deeper faith. Here's an example of what I mean. God wants to renew every aspect of every wound we suffer. Take the loss of my household, for instance. I loved my house in New England but had to admit it was defiled by the sins committed there.

I remember one afternoon shortly before the disclosure. I was emptying the washer and putting some clothes on the wooden drying rack that stood by the water heater. Finishing that, I looked up at the small window that was set high in the stone wall across the room. Light from the setting sun was falling through it in a clean shaft. Something about the light cutting through the dim cellar gave me pause. Then I dismissed it.

Later, after the truth about the crimes had come out, I was again folding clean clothes in the basement, and my traumatized thoughts began asking unanswerable questions. The basement was where my husband used to spend considerable time. It was the original man-cave. My frightened imagination wondered if his acts of violence had taken place close to the spot where I stood.

Returning in my memory to the image of the window with its light that I'd seen weeks before, I suddenly wondered if my daughter had ever looked up at it, and if she had, had it helped her? Victims report that focusing on a single object during the time they were being harmed helped them dissociate from the trauma. The idea of basements and cellars always made me anxious and sad after that thought, mostly because of what I didn't know. They triggered a stream of disturbing questions and fears.

Years later, I shared a prayer session with three other women for the purpose of healing traumatic feelings about the violence. Months after the session I realized that even the room where we prayed was used by the Holy Spirit to offer me solace. We were in the basement of our parish rectory. I recalled that at the start of the session I was asked to sit in a chair facing two high windows where the sun poured in. That thought triggered a memory about the basement back home. Remembering the depth and intensity of the prayer in that session, I had the sense that the wickedness that happened in our basement was overcome by God's love for us. He cleaned it out of the house and out of me and wanted me to know for certain that by bringing me back to the image I could now feel free of fear. The Lord is the Master of Life and will restore whoever comes to Him in whatever way He sees that they need it—no matter what they have done or what has been done to them.

God works outside of time. Triggers still occur in my life, but the grace to bear them has become even more powerful. One morning recently as I watched gently falling snowflakes in the chilly grey air it reminded me of the morning I drove to pick up my daughter in Vermont after she made the disclosure of abuse.

The plan was to bring her back home to make a report to police. It was about 6:00 a.m. when I entered the room in the log cabin where she had slept the night before. I knew she would be surprised to see me and I didn't want to startle her, so I quietly went up to her sleeping form and laid my hand on her back and whispered "good morning." She nearly jumped out of her skin.

"What are you doing here?" she demanded. Remembering the instructions I had received from the rape crisis counselor, I told her I knew what she said her father had done and that I believed her.

"Get *away* from me!" she screamed.

"What are you so mad at?" I asked her. My mind was reeling. "It's OK. We're going to get help. Dad has to go to jail."

"You don't know what you're talking about. It was all a lie. All of it. Now leave me alone!"

Then the house phone started to ring. It was the offender, yelling. He yelled that she was lying. He yelled that he would never do such a thing.

I hung up, over and over. This sequence of events was repeated until we finally got her things in the car and left. Fresh snow covered the piles that had already blanketed that mountain town. It was about 8:00 or 9:00 a.m. My only thought was that it was time for morning mass, but when I found the local church the people were already leaving. The ride back home was pure torture. My daughter was in a rage and all I could do was to try to refute what she said. I told her that her father was a criminal and had to face justice. She told me I was insane. All I could think was that I didn't know her or him any more. Fear, disgust, confusion all collided inside me. My instincts wanted to help and protect my child, and she was acting as though I were the enemy. Her hatred was a *spirit of Cruelty* cold as the snow surrounding us.

Today that spirit is being whittled away by the mercy of God. Persistent prayer is finding a way for me to become compassionate. It is making my heart new. The memories won't change, but their effect on me can. I'm trusting that God's plan to heal my relationship with my daughter will use the pain of the past like building blocks for a solid foundation to something loving and lasting between us.

If we stay frightened and hurt, we will frighten and hurt others. Instead, we can decide to find God in those painful moments and let Him bring us through it. If I'm focused on Him, I can't stay afraid for very long and I don't have to retaliate.

The Ultimate Weapon

Just as God is all love and desires nothing more than to live fully in each of His creatures, when we experience serious evil (and we remember evil is the great imitator) its *spirit of Fear* is the other power that wants to live in us. It isn't natural to trust what scares or confuses us, so we're often coerced by it instead. Trusting God, on the other hand, is trusting love, and love is never forced.

In the end, God is either everything or nothing. I was so frightened by what had happened in our family that for a long time I tried saying, "Sure, I trust You, Lord, so You've got to give me this and that." It was one long bargaining phase of grief. My trust in God, or anyone and everything else, became very conditional. Most of the people I talked to about the crime left God completely out of the ordeal, but I believe He either permits or ordains all things. So that had to mean sexual violence too. But how could it?

Saint Augustine said our souls are composed of the memory, intellect, and will. These are good gifts, so we can reason that our souls are drawn to what is good, the ultimate Good being God. When our souls are pleasing to God, we describe them as being in a state of grace. Grace keeps us close to God, and God is, essentially, love. Serious sin, on the other hand, involves not only the thoughts, words, or actions that make up the wrongdoing, but the negative spirits that are attached to these things. One of the reasons sexual violence is so damaging is that it creates a foothold for many powerful spirits: *spirits of Fear, Lies, and Chaos*, to name just a few.

These afflictions can be conquered by God's grace when we ask for it and cooperate with it. Like God Himself, grace is always available. It may not feel comfortable to think about God or evil and their involvement with this crime. It might make us angry or sad. If so, these are feelings God is permitting us to feel. He knows we have the gift of right reason to decide an appropriate way to respond to our feelings. If we allow feelings the power, they can distract and discourage us from receiving the great virtue of hope. If you don't feel able or willing to hope for God's goodness to enter into your experience, you can lift your mind and heart to Him with words like these: *Dear God, I don't know if I can dare to hope, but if it will help, let hope come to me.*

Being able to hear ourselves express what hurts and frightens us can give our broken trust a way to walk through the difficulty. When we offer the gift of listening, we lovingly imitate our God Who is always listening to us so He can come to our aid. How I wish I had been aware of this power when I was besieged with grief because I felt there was nothing I could do to help my daughter. Listening doesn't fix or judge. It loves. And then the love speaks, or not. My mother's example taught me this during the time I lived at her house. She listened to all my fear and distress and seemed to take it in as naturally as a wave pulls things in from the shore.

Sometimes we forget that Jesus is a Person we live with too. God became my closest confidant and He led me to another safe person and then another. As I began to allow myself to speak honestly about my feelings and thoughts, whether through prayer or in written form, my story eventually found its way into conversation with someone who would listen and then maybe offer their help. Relationships with trusted people are freer and deeper than others because we can give more of ourselves to them.

What do we get from taking the risk of sharing our darkness and pain? Well, what do we want?

Before performing a miracle, Jesus often asked this question of His petitioner. So I had to answer too. What did I want? I wanted peace. My peace-filled soul had become lost in a place where it felt impossible to love or be loved. This was making my life incomprehensible.

The poet Robert Frost wrote his understanding of our need to find and follow our inner light, that truth about what we know to be right and good. He said,

Our very life depends upon everything's
Recurring till we answer from within.[10]

This seems to say to me that all my experiences are threaded together. Each life event calls me to learn whatever lesson is there and then find a way to teach what I've received. That teaching is my answer. It could be something well or ill. Would revulsion be the main meat of my experience? Or could there be something else? If God is the Creator of all life and everything it contains, would I find something even in this experience worthy of coming from His hand?

What was "recurring" in me now was negative, angry, and afraid. How was I supposed to answer it? Only faith in an infinitely merciful Father Who wanted to heal me and my family made any sense. He wanted to give us a stronger love for Him, for ourselves, and for each other. It would be the flowering of His mercy in us. Yet the internal taunting that started in my head when the disclosure broke was now calling these thoughts idiotic dreams, *the same dreams you believed in the past, with all the other lies.* The supernatural power of the Evil One to deceive us in our thoughts and feelings can never be underestimated. No wonder Jesus advises us that what we hear in the dark, we must speak in the light (Matthew 10:17). We must learn to test the spirits.

Some of us want to believe the offender was trustworthy before we knew the truth about him. Just as often we want to condemn him when the truth is brought to light. These can be spiritually dangerous distractions regardless of how justified (or victimized) we may feel. What's important here is to see where God stands on the issue. Before any of us were born, when we were still a pure image in God the Father's Mind, He loved each of us infinitely. When we trust that love to be powerful enough to free us from any burden, it becomes the ultimate weapon.

For Reflection and Response ~

Do you feel you want to trust God more? If not, why?

If so, can you list three ways to do this?

How will more trust in Him become the ultimate weapon for you?

✦

৶৹৵

Surrender

৶৹৵

✦

2

I am sunk in the abysmal swamp
Where there is no foothold. I have reached the watery depths
The flood overwhelms me. (Psalm 69:3)

At the Jersey Shore, despite the feeling of safety afforded by being further away from the offender, my emotions were often unsteady. The loss of family life as I knew it brought on a loneliness that recalled a definition for it that I'd heard from a priest once. *Loneliness is not a feeling*, he said. *It's a state of soul.* My new normal was a desolation I couldn't explain or shake off. Unable to fix what had happened to us, I also didn't know how to accept it.

According to Raymond Flannery Jr., author of *Post-traumatic Stress Disorder: The Victim's Guide to Healing and Recovery*, when sexual violence happens within the family, it destroys our sense of place in that family. I felt I no longer belonged anywhere, because home wasn't safe for the victim or meaningful to me. And once disclosure blows his cover, it's no longer an advantage for the perpetrator either. Each of us is in exile inside and outside ourselves.

In prayer I had to ask, who would be more willing to meet us in that exile than the One Who remained faithful to the wandering Israelites? Or the One Who willingly went alone into the desert for 40 days to pray and fast before beginning His work of saving the world?

As I began to rely on God more and more, it was as though a floodgate opened. My feelings seemed centuries old. They woke up a new awareness of God's protection, not only for me but for the victims and the offender. If I believed in a God of love Who died on a cross for each of us, it meant there was nothing stronger that could stand against us. No matter how my experience of human love had been distorted or betrayed, I was loved forever by a perfect, all-powerful God. I needed to *find this love inside* myself and experience it in a tangible way. Most often it happened through the words of scripture or being in the presence of people who lived their faith. Then all I had to do was let it in. That idea seemed an impossible high-jump, unless I could surrender my grip on the false sense of control I tried to pass for daily living. My heart and mind were in tatters. I kept returning to the simple directives in the chant. Surrender. What was it and how did I do it?

One description of surrender says that it is an act of the will when it consents to go through something. As a non-offender I felt compelled to meet my daughter and her offender in their misery and somehow bring them to God's care. This had to be the merciful thing to do. Looking up from my own wounds became the act of offering prayer for my family. It was a petition for grace and forgiveness even as it was a grace to receive the desire to ask for it. This action of grace was nothing I could control or maneuver; I could only surrender to my need of it.

Buried Alive

While kneeling in confession, I was shocked when the priest practically congratulated me. "You're fortunate you can feel your feelings. Most people can't. The more disturbing our feelings are, the more we want to put them away from us. *"You should thank God. It's a gift to be able to feel them."* Terror, anxiety, disbelief, confusion, anger: these were just a handful of my feelings after the disclosure. What about you?

When someone involved with abuse can recall the episodes but not the feelings they felt in connection with them, psychologists call that response "an isolation of affect." It is in such cases that the victim may become a victimizer, because the effect of what they suffered can't be completely repressed. Often it will seek to be released through re-enacting the violence. This return to the cycle of abuse is part of the failure to control an interior strife that cries out from the soul to be surrendered.

No matter how we've experienced sexual violence, it leaves our feelings at risk. If we don't get the support to face our pain with trust that it can be resolved with God, most of us will opt to self-protect. Our choices for doing this are often an addiction, compulsive lying, rage, or another abusive behavior. Flannery notes that over 80 percent of criminals incarcerated for sexual violence and 50 percent of violent crimes in households are related to drug or alcohol abuse. So escape is part of the cycle. Running away, in whatever addictive form it takes, makes us feel like we're doing something. It eases the tension of feeling trapped in our suffering.

Chronic suffering from the effects of sexual violence can be fed by denial of a basic spiritual truth. With the promise of Heaven, we are destined for a love that has no end. Sexual violence thrives on distorting our ideas and beliefs about love and what love has the power to do. Sexual violence has nothing to do with love, except that only God's love can completely heal us from its injuries.

Residual feelings can lie dormant when covered with time until they get a spiritual tap on the shoulder—like Linda did when she began practicing her faith as an older adult. She described herself as the sort of woman who was willing to help others but wouldn't admit she needed help too. *"I wasn't aware I was numb. Outside I was very huggy. My first clue was in the prayer community called Women Ministering to Women. When they prayed and laid hands on me, under the numbness was negative emotion."*

With prayer and support we can decide to surrender pain from an inner wound by giving it to God. One preliminary way to do this is to use what's called a *God Box*. It enables a simple but profound act of surrender and works like this. Find or create a container of any size. It can be whatever appeals to you as a place to put an offering to God. Then, when a troubling issue keeps intruding on your peace, briefly write down what it is. You can use words or a drawing. It can be as simple as a name, a symbol, or a date—whatever describes what you're feeling. Remember that God already knows all the details. Then fold the piece of paper slowly and carefully. Once you drop it in the God Box, you've let it go. I've often been surprised when emptying my God box from time to time. I'll read the slips of paper only to discover I can barely remember the issue that was connected with their content. That's how freeing it is.

For some of us, this silent surrender can be the first time we've reached out to God in a while—or maybe the first time ever. The silence shared with the Lord at this time can be healing too. Since it's part of the ministry of the Church to expel evil spirits, it makes a holistic approach to our healing possible and necessary. Inner restoration takes place in stages: first the body, then the mind, then the emotions.

In the beginning I wasn't aware of how much fear I carried inside. I was too ashamed and angry. Continuing to lift my heart to God in various forms of prayer, I kept being reminded of the passage *"I make all things new"* (Revelations 21:5). It was an intriguing offer, but for a long time I clung to my own list of wants. Irritated and impatient, I often rebelled, saying *I don't deserve all this pain.* But once, when I could quiet the inner complaints long enough, I could sense a reply to them all. It simply asked *who does?* How I answered that gentle question would mean either a return to my torment or a chance for rebirth. That answer from within, as Robert Frost noted, is our ultimate, unstoppable gift of free will.

The Shame Factor

Perhaps the most potent weapon *against* breaking the cycle of violence is shame—especially shame that remains long after the active violence ends. Shame can be so debilitating it will mute our innermost understanding of who we are and what we mean to God. We hang our heads under its yoke. Walking in the same shoes as shame is our choice of resistance, the *spirit of Rage* or *Wrath*.

Rage is not to be confused with legitimate anger, anger that desires not violence against the offender but restitution for wrongs (CCC 2302). Why make such a distinction in cases as blatantly evil as these? Wrath isn't looking for justice but to harm another. If allowed, vengeful rage will take on perpetual motion in the human condition. It is a sin with deep, thick roots. Saint Paul warns us not to let the sun go down on our anger (Ephesians 4:26) as a means of cutting off the entrance to this deadly stronghold. Violence breeds violence. When the rage exhausts us there's shame to take its place.

Involvement in sex crimes can make us ashamed of ourselves, of offenders we loved or trusted, of non-offenders we thought we could count on, of our imagined loss of innocence, and of a thousand other hurtful beliefs. At these times we need to remember that although the war under our skin is real as rain, we have an Advocate, the Holy Spirit, Who will give us the gifts of knowledge and wisdom. He will come to our defense and win.

One survivor of the priestly scandals revealed in Pennsylvania recently was quoted as saying that she felt "Everything they taught me was a lie. Besides my faith in God, I don't know what to believe anymore." This clear expression of the turmoil inflicted by the evil attached to the violence can also be used as a light by which we can see our path toward healing. Naming the spirits we need to be freed from is an essential in regaining our freedom.

Fr. Ralph A. DiOrio, a Catholic priest who had an international healing ministry based in Massachusetts, said, *"Evil only wants one thing: our minds. If it gets that, the rest will follow."* This warning helped me stay on alert when my thinking got obsessed with what my husband had done, and where, when, and why. It was dangerous ground, but there was further instruction: *"The Devil and his angels,"* says Fr. Basil Nortz, *"use our imagination for a foothold in order to corrupt the intellect with thoughts that don't hold any truth."*[11] This can be fought, he says, by silencing the imagination and bringing it to God in the depths of our soul where a holy silence can grow.

The act of bringing things to God is one way to understand surrender that will help us clear out unwanted attachments. Shame stigmatizes, angers, and frightens us with its pure power to whittle our peace to a trembling core. It thrives on keeping us focused on ourselves, because in a spiritual sense, it is rooted in pride. Only we can shame ourselves. What others say or think about us doesn't have to dictate our reaction.

While meeting with my pastor to share some healing prayer, I remember telling him how overwhelmed I felt because of what had happened in my family. *"I'm so ashamed,"* I said. It seemed an odd thing for me to admit, because I thought only the primary victims suffered from shame, and I didn't see myself as one of them. Shame was showing its wide and welcoming borders. *When non-offenders don't take action even after they've been informed about an incident of abuse, shame is often part of the reason why.* There is shame about what was done and shame over not knowing what to do about it. These are crippling feelings that can render us unwilling or unable to reach out for help.

When our disclosure first came out, having no words to reference the profound impact of its darkness, I went to God's Word for help in sorting it out. The image that struck me at that point was the concept of an "enemy." I never imagined myself having any. How foolish. With reflective prayer it was clear to see how *each of us is infinitely hated by evil.* It wants to conquer our human will, and has legions ready to try to do it. Each member of those legions is expert at convincing us to think in a way that will secure their victory best. Often it's as simple as getting us to *underestimate it.* If we do that, we won't see the constant need to be on our guard.

I completely underestimated the design of evil against what it knows belongs to God. And what do strong enemies do? They attack from all sides. The most efficient strategy is to get the enemy to crumble from within. Fear-filled shame is a prime tool for the job.

Shame, with its self-centeredness, is a false god. My shame seemed to bind me to self-pity. The crimes inflicted such a deep stigma that I often couldn't allow myself to accept sympathy from caring friends. Doing so only made me feel even more inadequate. I believed I'd failed as a parent and a spouse, and that inflicted a deep humiliation. It made me feel angry, suspicious, and stifled. At the same time I continued to seek the Lord's wisdom. To accept God's infinite care for us is to see our value in His eyes. When God values something, it's good. In the light of that truth, shame can be lifted from us by hope.

The gift of hope isn't a one-time fix, however—wars involve many battles. At times my inner darkness was so thick all I could understand about my shame was that it left me desolate, feeling that God was absent. Then the shame would flip over into pride. Self-righteousness wanted to condemn the others involved for their decisions, when by faith I knew that judgment is God's alone.

Limping between shame and pride created an emotional dependency that wanted to replace my genuine worship of God. In my prayer at times there seemed no path to the good and gentle Jesus Who died for love of me. My thoughts were preoccupied with the fact that this crime triumphed in my household even as I was trying to live a committed life of faith. Only the Lord had the light to see by, and He wanted nothing more than to bring us all into it. I was struggling within myself on levels totally unfamiliar and frightening. When I admitted feeling ashamed during that appointment with my pastor, I'm sure he began to silently pray against it, because by the time I left, I felt freed to decide what to do.

Christian counselor R. Thomas Brass explains that shame uses loneliness as a shield, but as a result those who are shamed

forfeit love.[12] Shame can let me feel I'm in control of the punishment that's due me. That means I'm trying to do the work
Christ has already done. Clinging to my shame, I'm refusing to
allow God to count me as one of the saved. If shame isn't used
as a springboard to repentance, it's prideful, and pride is a cor-
nerstone of sin. Brass reminds us that it's not easy to let go of
pride and shame, but both can be banished by the virtue of humility. To see ourselves as God sees us is what it means to be
humble. Although we can't give humility to ourselves, it is a
gift freely given by God when we repent our wrongdoing and
ask Him for it.

God will often answer our prayers, especially those asking
for spiritual blessings like virtues, by giving us graces. In the
language of Saint Ignatius's spirituality, we can ask God for *the
grace of shame* and watch how it will transform us. Saint Ignatius
of Loyola is said to have asked for this grace as he prayed in
front of a crucifix before making his confession. The grace of
shame embodies a gift of humility that calls us to examine all
the ways we are distracted and rebel against the love of God.

When we experience shame without the reassurance of
God's love for us, a spiritual vacuum is created where sin can
thrive, often serious sin. Humility is known as the queen of virtues since the perfection of all the others depends on the
strength of a humble soul. Neither fear nor sin can hold sway
for long in the lives of those who are truly humble. If the grace
of shame can help us grow in humility, there is more than hope
after sexual violence; there's a chance for joy.

A Harvest for All

Prayer is the bounty of a loving heart. It is the solace of a broken
one. We pray most often at first when we're afraid or confused,

because underneath those feelings is a sense of lost love. Jesus constantly prays for us. Saint Paul instructs us to do the same thing in his first letter to the Thessalonians (5:16–18), but what does it mean to pray always, and what will it do for us? Prayer helps us be renewed and transformed in our minds (Romans 20:2) so we can see each other as beloved children of the Father. Prayer is meant to lead to action. Often, I get help from prayer to do something positive about negative things.

After the disclosure my prayer was mostly telling God what I wanted and needed, varied only with asking Him "why" about my ordeal and all its repercussions. This wasted a lot of emotional energy and clarity of mind. Obstinately asking to know *why* really means I want the answer that I want, not the one I'm getting. I'd often argue with God. Then I'd weep when He ministered to me through scripture that mysteriously and directly comforted my tortured heart.

Even the *desire* to pray is an inspiration from the Holy Spirit. It's like the Mother's Day coupon my daughter clipped from the newspaper when she was ten. It entitled the bearer to one free rose from the florist shop up the street. When I found the coupon sitting on a table in the living room, I asked her about it. She suddenly looked a little sad, and said, *"Oh, I wanted to get it for you."* Although Mother's Day had already passed, I told her how happy it made me feel to think she wanted to do something so sweet. I've kept the coupon with its line drawing of a long-stem red rose ever since. It's tucked in my Bible like a real rose would be, because to me it is real. Her intention made it real.

If such an incident can give a sinner like me the delight that it did, how God must thrill at even our most awkward attempts at prayer and praise. *"When you pray, go to your inner room…and pray to your Father...and your Father will repay you"* (Matthew 6:6). Our Father God *wants* to hear us pray to Him in private and in community. *"Indeed, the Father seeks those who will pray to Him"* (John 4:23), Jesus told the Samaritan woman at the well. Our Father, Papa, is seeking us so we will pray to Him—imagine that. In the letter to the Hebrews, Saint Paul says that because of His reverence in prayer, Jesus *"was heard"* (Hebrews 6:7). This simple phrase lets us see how much love there is in being heard. If we let the reverence Jesus had as He prayed to His Father become a model for us, we can be sure we'll be heard too. This is praying with faith.

According to Rev. Joseph Bucik, an American Baptist clinical pastoral chaplain and supervisor at the Adult Diagnostic and Treatment Center in Avenel, New Jersey, about 40% of the inmates there use religion as a perspective on their sentencing. *"I try to encourage them to commit to what their faith teaches,"* he said, *"so that their actions can be consonant with their faith. Faith means action."* As we grow in our faith, we learn to take our life to prayer and our prayer to life. The following are a few different ways prayer changes things.

Private Prayer

Scripture spoke to my heart about exactly what I was facing in the aftermath of sexual violence. That is the power of the living Word. Because God doesn't change in the tumult of life, we have hope He will bring us to meaningful and joyful living whenever we let Him enter our experience. He tells us in the book of Revelation, *"Behold, I stand at the door and knock. If anyone hears my voice and opens the door then I will enter"* (Revelation 3:20). Prayer will guide and strengthen us to let Him in more fully. Meditating on the life and love of the Lord gave me new meaning where chaos wanted to reign, and peace to calm my heart.

In the novel *The Color Purple*, the main character, Celie, in her grief after being raped by a family member, begins to write letters to God. In them she releases her anguish and builds her trust in a loving Lord Who she hopes will rescue her. The letters become her form of prayer. As she matures, she finds the strength to walk in the truth of her own goodness, the goodness she searched for in those letters.

Keeping a prayer journal has been part of my faith life for years, but since I joined a group of intercessors at our parish, we direct our writing to the Person of God the Father. We address Him the same way Jesus taught His disciples—as Abba, or Papa. This deepens the intimacy in our meditations. I come before Papa as my loving Father and God, also knowing He is the great I AM (Exodus 3:14). A relationship like this may seem unappealing to those who have been hurt by their earthly fathers, by clergy, or by a male authority figure they trusted like a father. It can make us feel angry at God for what we suffered. But I desperately needed to put my inner life in right order, and who better to ask for help in doing that than the great I AM? He is the only Perfect Father.

And when I turn to the all-powerful God also as my loving Pa, it compels me to hope He will be merciful, show me His will, and share His wisdom about what happened to us. Daily meditation and journaling on scripture brought out where I was inside myself and where God wanted me to be. The road to inner peace would be as long as the time it took to surrender each conflict to God's will. Sin and God cannot live in the same house.

Asking Papa how He sees our prayers to Him helped me persevere. *Pray, my child. Pray and know the way. Pray and* you will do My will. In prayer you will find your rest, and in this rest you will perform the work of your life with sweet wisdom as your guide. Children want to follow when they are learning. You are learning how to return to Heaven.

Adoration

Adoration chapels are located throughout the world.[13] In these places the exposed consecrated Bread or Host is what Catholics believe to be the Body, Blood, Soul, and Divinity of Jesus Christ. The Host is displayed in a monstrance or vessel used for veneration. Adoration of the Eucharist or Blessed Sacrament can be attended by a large group of people or only a handful. Sometimes you have the joy of being alone with Him. Our form prayer in the Presence of the God can be a combination of spoken litanies, songs, or meditations; but perhaps the most poignant is silent and wordless adoration.

Prayer reaches past any obstacle, especially prayer offered in the Name of Jesus and said in the company of His Eucharistic Presence. There is prayer that asks and prayer that thanks or praises. When we lay these aside and go to the Lord just to be embraced by Him, we meet Him in freedom. As the father of the prodigal son *"saw him a long way off,"* so our Father God sees us, every hour, every day. Even now His gaze searches with unspeakable longing until we turn to adore Him. Here, in this place of adoration before the Blessed Sacrament, He is the Almighty, in what looks like a piece of bread.

A friend describes her experience of being in the Presence of Christ during adoration as a personal sensation: *"Just sitting there you can feel the bad going out and the good coming in."* Many hours spent in the adoration chapel built up a reservoir of strength beneath my brokenness. It's not everyone who can walk into a room and see the Eternal God before them. The privilege of doing so is a mystery of His love for us, no matter who we are. For me, it's an experience that never gets old. I learned that a small group of inmates, convicted sex offenders at Avenel Prison, are also familiar with the graces given during Adoration. When I try to picture them sitting in front of the exposed Host, the mercy of God suddenly becomes very real.

Sitting or kneeling before the Presence of Jesus exposed in the Eucharist, in the absence of any community prayer service, individuals maintain a respectful silence. Such silence is a strong ally when seeking inner surrender. Through this holy silence God turns the tables on one of the most insidious aspects of active sexual violence: *the mute spirit* (Mark 9:25). The Lord holds out an invitation to share a deep exchange with the humble soul who is willingly silent in adoration before Him. Meditating on scripture in the Presence of the Eucharist can reveal His truth and promises in unimaginable ways. Our silence shared with God opens up a channel of comfort when we enter it. It is a place where our spirit is uninhibited, becoming first and always His beloved child. In time, this identity strengthens and blossoms. It becomes our signal call from paradise to turn our hearts ever more closely to His. We are no longer silenced by fear or intimidation, but instead a peace the world cannot give fills us to overflowing.

In the adoration chapel all my unanswered questions eventually settle down. Jesus tells us He is *"the way, the truth, and the life"* (John 14:6). This ignites my cold and frightened faith. It calls me to bring out the lies from my wounds and lay them before Him. He will help me discern my confusion from the stockpiles of fear. Together we sort through lies like these with the wisdom of His Holy Spirit:

—That it's impossible to experience joy after sexual violence;
—That it was my fault I didn't know about the crimes happening to others;
—That the perpetrator is hopelessly afflicted and the victims will never fully recover;
—That the problem is not transferable to compassionate dialogue;
—That the scars are a stigma to be hidden;
—That I am alone in my shame;
—That there's no anger sufficient to punish those responsible;
—That there's no justice for what I've suffered.

If you don't believe in the real Presence of Christ in the Eucharistic Host, you can ask for the grace to believe. He puts Himself before us in the everlasting hope we will do exactly that. Over time hearts are transformed before Him. Why miss the opportunity? Witness the beauty of others wrapped in their worship if you haven't found your own way yet. Let the community inside the chapel give you silent strength with their faith. When you share your silence with Him, He will talk to you. This is prayer from the depths of His love. For me, it never fails to be a time of very deep healing.

The Mass

The mass is considered by Catholics to be "the greatest prayer" and is uniquely both an individual and communal encounter with Christ. Churches in large cities often have several daily masses scheduled, so if you've never been to one, why wait? Books of prayer called missals are usually available in the pews or nearby and provide the spoken responses and the day's readings.

Even though I'd attended daily mass for years before the disclosure, afterwards there was a difference in how I heard the prayers. They became the words of my Friend, urging me to remain in His love and keep my heart close to the truth in His Word. Slowly, I saw my helplessness because of our situation not as a curse or a stigma but as a deepening in my soul that brought me to a new place of security in God. It was another place of surrender. I would enter church for mass with nothing but tension where my heart used to be, and at the conclusion I'd leave renewed and strengthened.

Attending mass and receiving the Eucharist *"brings a certain peace and awareness of a need to change,"* said Fr. Mike Scott, who was then a volunteer at Avenel Prison for sex offenders. It's there that a core group of prisoners bring themselves and others into an active practice of their faith. *"Every week guys go to mass and receive the Eucharist. They say the meditative prayer of the Rosary and see Mary as a model of purity."*

One weekday during mass, at the time of consecration I received an inspired prayer. It's become the way I pray for our offender every day. When the priest asks God our Father to bless the bread and wine so they will become the Body and Blood of Christ, he first takes the bread or host and prays over it using the words Christ did at the Last Supper. Then he picks up the chalice and prays, *"Take this all of you and drink from it, for this is the chalice of My Blood, the Blood of the new and eternal covenant, which will be poured out for you and for many for the forgiveness of sins. Do this in memory of Me."* Then he lifts the chalice for us to venerate. At that time I silently pray the following words: "I immerse myself into the cup of Your Precious Blood, Lord. I immerse also all the souls You have put on my heart. Heal us. Restore us. Have mercy on us. *I ask this even unto my last enemy.*" This prayer teaches me that we keep our loved ones and our enemies in the same place. The Lord is impartial in every way.

Our prayer can reach past any obstacle. After the Host is consecrated, the priest says, *"Behold the Lamb of God Who takes away the sins of the world. Happy are those who are called to His supper."* For a long time I meditated on that prayer. Where does Jesus take the sins of the world? And why didn't I feel free of the effects from the sins of the offender? Evil had a ready response to those questions, wanting me to believe about Christ's sacrifice, *"that was then, but this is now."* But if that were true, the mass would have no value. In His sacrifice on Calvary Christ willingly took our sins upon Himself, for all time. How does the Lamb take our sins away when sin continues to thwart and cripple us? His passion and death more than obliterate the effects of all sin. He takes our war between good and evil into His own Body and Blood so that we can choose to freely walk into His life and live there, just as He chose to pick up our human life and sanctify it. Discovering this mystery of God's love and clinging to it is a gift of God's mercy in itself.

Every time I wrestle with thoughts concerned with the evil inflicted on us because of sexual crimes, it brings me face-to-face with *"a hideous strength,"* as C. S. Lewis called it. I need goodness to shield me when facing my inner disorder and hurt. Knowing that perpetrators are mentally ill (to the extent that evil wounds our minds) can only lead me to a good if it serves as a call to have mercy on them. Is that even possible? Not by my power, but mercy is always granted to a contrite heart. I began to ask God to have mercy on me and began to pray for my enemies as though my life depended on it, which it actually does. If I can't forgive, and even learn to bless them, my heart will be bound by the burden.

One afternoon as I sat resting in the pew after mass, I began to pray for our offender, and these were the words that came to me: *After 30 years of trying to love you, I've finally found the way. It is in knowing who you truly are, begging God for mercy because of it, and receiving that mercy into my own heart.* Mercy is love. And isn't this the way we can come to love *ourselves* in the end?

Community Prayer

Psychologists say that feelings of isolation that stem from the blame, despair, and shame involved in sex crimes can give us a self-concept of "specialness." It's not a positive state of mind, but one that says *No one will ever understand what I've lived through. No one cares what I've suffered.* We feel utterly alone because there's no pain greater than ours. This can translate into attitudes that used to be called having a chip on one's shoulder or thinking of oneself as God's gift to the human race.

As people who have been hurt by sexual violence, we can see our participation at the gathering to celebrate mass as a way to let go of our specialness. We can surrender our need to feel in control by remaining separate or aloof, and instead, let God's blessings come to us through His Body during worship. Shared song and prayer can do much to peel away anxiety. It took quite a while for me to surrender my need to think I could control my daughter's choices for her healing. I feared if she didn't reach for God's help, it wasn't going to happen, but that isn't entirely true. Sometimes we can't act in our own best interest, and God knows that. At these times His merciful grace can come to us from the prayer of those who love us or even from total strangers.

Years before our disclosure there was a woman who went to the same morning mass I did, and she offered a personal prayer of petition that only struck me as compassionate at the time, nothing more.

This woman spoke up every morning with the same request: *"May the Lord guide the care and safety of all the battered and abused children in the world."* Neither she nor I knew then how those words would support me later, and if they helped me, what did they do for my daughter?

Going to mass remains my front line of defense. In the early days of my grief and for a long time afterwards, as soon as the mass ended I wanted it to begin again. It was the closest glimpse of heaven I could have. The readings from scripture, homilies, and Holy Communion fortify my thinking and my will to fight the hopelessness always lurking in the unresolved hurt from the crimes. It was humbling to hear that convicted sex offenders share in that struggle. *"When they say the Confiteor prayer at the start of mass,"* Fr. Scott explained, *"it begins with the words 'I confess.' This is a public admission of personal responsibility. It sums up everything, and it's communal. I need to ask for their help too."* From that foundation of trust the men are able to share on a more individual level, Fr. Scott said. *"This week ten guys admitted they were molested by priests as youngsters. They were able to speak on letting go of anger. It's impressive to hear them pray for their own victims before mass. It was their idea. Honesty comes with that."*

The mass is how we remember Christ gave His life and death for us so we can be free: free of lies and the wounds they cause. I don't know how this happens—only that it does, over and over again.

Deliverance, Healing, and Discernment

Whether we're aware of it or not, we suffer injuries every day. Someone cuts us off in traffic. A coworker mutters under his breath after we've had some words with him. A friend misunderstands us on an issue that's difficult to share. Psychologists say we need 12 hugs a day to feel stable and loved. Part of the spiritual means to good health is prayer, of course, and when our injuries are serious, the prayer must be too.

Stress can overwhelm our bodies and cause physical discomfort or disease. The same is true for our souls. When the violence of serious sin distorts our inner world, it takes much grace to find our way back to joy again. Grace and strength are ever available by asking for them in prayer. When we turn to trusted others to pray for us or with us, we can be sure our asking is energized and directed by the Holy Spirit. This is the experience of intercessory prayer.

Healing prayer and deliverance are forms of intercession. We've already looked at Theophostic prayer and found it both heals and delivers the petitioner from lie-based pain. Christianity has other forms of deliverance prayer, and it's important to find one for the support and discernment they can offer us. If group prayer is not something you can consider because of past experiences, individual prayer from a priest or Christian counselor can be equally powerful. The graces from the Holy Spirit received through healing, and deliverance prayer with its gifts of prophecy and words of knowledge can bring forth the fruit of promises such as those found in the passages of Ezekiel's "dry bones": *"O my people! I will put my spirit in you that you may live"* (Ezekiel 37:1–14). That passage is a wonderful promise of personal resurrection and renewal.

As life-giving and calming as healing prayer often is, it also acts as a purifying power in our mind and emotions. It's not uncommon for someone experiencing healing prayer to have a sudden urge to cry, even though they may not feel sad. This might sound contradictory, but it's a working of the Holy Spirit called the gift of tears, a spontaneous and penetrating sense of God's loving Presence in our hearts. His Presence is allowing us to release some inwardly held perceptions or feelings that may have kept us from receiving all the healing love Christ has for us.

Prayer from the Lord's community, whether it's from one person or several, offers us the strength of united others coming together in faith before the Lord on our behalf. An action of the Holy Spirit during healing prayer is when a person receives a word of knowledge to share with us. Soon after our disclosure while I was still living in New England, a friend who was in a faith-sharing group with me said she received two passages from scripture while praying for my daughter and me. One was the prophecy of Simeon, who told the Blessed Mother on the day she presented her Son in the temple, *"A sword shall pierce your own heart too, so that the thoughts of many might be laid bare"* (Luke 2:35). The other was an image of the mockery of Christ by the soldiers. My friend reminded me that the passage says *"the whole cohort"* was gathered around Him. *"He suffered every sin and trial that afflicts us." "And,"* she said gently, *"sexual violence is included in that"* (Matthew 27:27).

No matter what our crisis, Jesus and His mother have been there. When He cast out demons from the people around Him, certainly some of them were demons attached to sins of sexual violence. Jesus goes with us everywhere, and He can go right now. Seeing the Lord as a Person Who wants to be our support and advocate is an unfamiliar offer for many of us. The stigma of having experienced sexual violence works deep in us to isolate and separate us, even from ourselves.

"We have to stop believing as a society that these crimes are dirty and we'll be contaminated if we get involved. Scripture says only the inside contaminates. Fear of the sin causes the hiding which strengthens the evil," Linda Whalen claims. God gave Linda courage and reminded her that He places a desire inside all of us to please Him. She realized as she practiced her faith that she never lost that desire. With support from her faith community she understood that "God wants to walk with us. You have to let Him in. You never see around the corner at what He'll do. You have to go on faith."

That's often easier said than done. If you're in the grip of fear about how God may treat you, you can fight it with something as simple as placing a prayer request on a website such as the Lourdes prayer request site listed in the resources at the back of this book. Or, you can hear the healing words of Fr. Ralph DiOrio recorded on YouTube. There are also hotlines where you can remain anonymous if you're a victim or a predator who wants to stop offending on StopItNow.org.

I didn't know what to expect when I first started to receive intercessory prayers from others but it has always helped. Here's an example. To receive prayer or spiritual insight from those who have the gift of discernment means the Holy Spirit allows that person certain knowledge in the spiritual realm (Acts 16:16–18, 1 Corinthians 12:10). When we meet regularly with other Christians for prayer, sharing a word of knowledge becomes a frequent and natural exercise of a spiritual gift. Because this gift is rooted in the Holy Spirit, it comes from love—and love is what heals us.

One Sunday after mass I went to the back of the church to receive intercessory prayer from two other women in the parish. I didn't share any specific information with them about the crimes, but left it up to the Lord to speak through their focused prayer. We united our hearts for my intentions, they placed their hands on my head and shoulders, and these are some the words they shared: *"The battle is old. Just like He was there for Moses, He will be at your side too. He will give you joy. He's waiting for you to welcome Him."* And then this: *"There is a darkness covering you like a kind of death. And then there is a light shooting out of the tabernacle like a sword, and it will cut through the darkness. It's darkness like before Jesus was born. Be patient. He will come."*

A new foundation was being built in me even as the temptations to fear for my daughter's well-being got stronger. This is the spiritual battle Linda talked about. Over time I understood that our healing doesn't take away the difficulty of carrying our cross. Spiritual healing diminishes our fear and confusion in picking it up. Carrying a cross is not a punishment; it's a privilege, because Christ did it first and asks us to follow Him. The purpose is always Heaven.

Confession

Frequent confession releases God's healing in us at its peak. Confession is a sacrament, but if you're not Catholic, you can still see a priest for counsel or just to be heard. Caring for souls is a priest's job description, and it's been my experience that most of them do it very well. The offer of a listening heart is beyond price. For those who have suffered because of sexual violence, it's a safe place to tell our story.

At this point in time many could argue with the statements above. But I believe the Lord is exposing the secrecy and strength of worldwide sexual violence during these days in order to purify the sinful who repent and console the traumatized who mourn, as we let the Him enter our experience with His mercy.

Each of us is created to be a temple of the Holy Spirit. This calls us to live lives that will nurture our growth in holiness. When we deny this truth about ourselves by sinning, especially sinning against our purity, we need help to turn from those ways with full sorrow and reparation. What usually happens is a deepening of silence and deceit around the crimes and those involved. Now, in this present culture, people finally have ears to hear the truth. Knowing what Christ would have us do when reports are found credible can finally expand our goals beyond punitive justice to include the wisdom of who we are as His children. This is a special calling for non-offenders. We can participate with God to help transform the broken-hearted by becoming agents of His healing love even as we are being healed.

Since sexual violence is dominated by the darkness of *arrogance,* our exposure to it can victimize us no matter how we were involved with the crime. Under its influence I can make demands on others, myself, and God that are wrong and selfish. I can become blind or complacent about my responsibilities. *"The person's biggest torture, whether they are the victim or the offender, is that they're separated from God,"* says Linda.

It can be difficult to accept that a person victimized as a child is then to see him or herself as a sinner in any way, but Linda is clear on this point. Feelings of guilt in sexual assault victims are common and often overwhelming after disclosure. This guilt is fed by memories of the offender or even by family members or others who assert that the child is somehow to blame. Serious sins corrupt the mind and emotions with extraordinary power. In order to heal on this deep level our thoughts and feelings must be made new. Linda's prayer and the Lord's revelation gently let her see the patterns in her life where she fostered wrong choices. While she was in no way guilty of the assaults she suffered, in order for her to access the healing that God wanted to come to her, she first had to take responsibility for all her sinful choices and resentments.

In her book, Linda writes about an incident when she was a teenager, after she had already been deeply hurt by sexual violence. One night she went to a drive-in movie with her brother's trusted friend—who then raped her. The boy said to her afterward, *"You must hate me,"* and she answered no, that she actually felt nothing. She realized later that she had developed *"the worst kind of layer inside me: numbness, and indifference to sin."*[14]

Later in life, with prayer and the sacraments, things changed for Linda. "Anger would knot me up inside," she remembers. "Now the knot is gone completely. I enjoy every moment. I go immediately to my Father. That freedom is there for every wounded person. You can't stop at being a survivor, understand the pain. Let Jesus remove the scar tissue. God wants every soul back with Him. Do I want to work with Him or against Him by carrying hate? Where do I want to be? Pleasing God or wishing suffering for the sinner? The answer will show where our freedom lies."

Making a good confession starts with good preparation. When we remember that negative feelings are a foothold for negative words and actions, prayer about them can turn out to be a deep examination of conscience. *Confession holds me accountable to change my behavior* while at the same time strengthens me to make better decisions. Confession is not a put-down. It means I want to change and will have the grace to support this desire. God's grace is infinite, and it's never denied to those who ask for it in truth. But many of us won't be convinced of the need to go before a priest to expose our interior world. We use the reasoning that "I talk to God. He knows I'm sorry." For me, going to confession gives me a sense of having received a lightness of soul afterward. It's a supernatural gift that I can't compare to anything else.

One resource I've found to be excellent in the examination of our conscience is a talk by Bishop Robert Barron called *The Seven Deadly Sins, Seven Lively Virtues*. It's a thought-provoking and informative look at our struggles with sin and the dysfunctional behaviors resulting from them. Each capital sin is connected with a virtue and some practical ways to cultivate it.

Until I acknowledge my feelings and take responsibility for what they indicate, I can't hope to gain control of them. For instance, if I'm trapped in self-condemnation because I didn't prevent the harm done to my child, that blame doesn't benefit anyone. It means I'm angry, frightened, and probably wanting revenge. Blame is never from God. Blame damages or kills relationships, even the one I have with myself.

These thoughts must be resolved with faith in *Christ*, Who *"by the blood of his cross in his own person killed the hostility and reconciled men with God"* (CCC 2305). If blame is never from God, why do we sometimes feel so guilty about our wrongdoing? Is there a difference between guilt and contrition? One understanding is that guilt is from the Evil One and contrition is from the Lord. The first accuses and condemns while the second brings remorse that leads to repentance. Evil is a murderer. God gives us new life.

There's a sense of unity in the fact that we're all sinners. This means I must love myself despite my failings because that is what God does, and I must love others too—all others. This is only possible through God's love, which is alive and active in me through His grace. You may be familiar with the phrase "hurt people hurt people." When I let my hurt become hurtful to others I'm at fault regardless of the root cause. An example would be to become angry because of someone's anger toward me. But if my anger causes me to retaliate or hate another, it becomes my wrongdoing.

In the end we will be personally accountable to God for our disposition and our actions, as we pray in the Confiteor, "in what I have done, and what I have failed to do." Faith helps me find peace in God because He is our protector. It's important to note here that protection and prevention are two different things. God didn't prevent the violence in my house, but His endless love will protect us so we can return to Him through all the fallout.

If you are at the point where you're ready to acknowledge your own errors, but the fear of confessing them is holding you back from seeing a priest, try to keep your concentration on the grace you'll receive from the sacrament. Grace is spiritual strength. Hopefully your anticipation of this gift will help you summon the courage to seek out God's mercy. The priest is a mere human endowed with the graces of the sacrament of Holy Orders. He is ordained to guide and assure souls of their worth in the Creator's Heart.

Priests fall short just as we do. If a negative encounter with a priest in confession leaves you more concerned with the per-sonality of the priest than with God's message to you that should be coming through him, find another priest to speak with. Here's an example of what I mean.

During the most difficult times, God's grace led me to compassionate priests who offered valuable discernment during confession. It wasn't always sympathetic, however—like the time Fr. Lane responded to my confession of anger against one of the survivors who treated me with cruelty and contempt. I saw it as a second round of deep betrayal and hoped for his understanding as well as forgiveness for my outrage about it. The priest listened to my story quietly and then asked, *"Who do you think put that anger inside you?* And before I could take a breath to speak he snapped, *"You did!"*

It caught me off guard but I had to own it. In an instant it made the cause of my latest anxieties clear and lifted me past another brush with self-pity. That evening, still reeling a bit, I reasoned with myself: *Sure, you were hurt, even persecuted. But you don't have to be bitter and vindictive. You're going to be accountable for your actions and attitudes. You have no power over others. Don't act as though you do.*

I was taught to always say a quick prayer to the Holy Spirit before making my confession so that my heart would be contrite. It always seems to work well. In this particular incident I felt relieved I confessed the sin and received the guidance I needed. There is a holy path laid out here for us having to do with the first commandment that says we are not to have any gods before the Lord our God.

My fallen nature consistently wants to supersede God with my own will, my own agenda. But He alone is Lord, and when I can live that, holiness can increase. One help for living a strong faith is to believe in God's infinite desire to save us, to forgive us our wrongs.

Listen to the words of Saint Ambrose, the Archbishop of Milan who baptized Saint Augustine. He said, *"The offense did us more good than harm, because it gave divine mercy the opportunity to redeem us."*[15] When we apply those words to the crime of sexual violence, they become superbly challenging and yet, for me at least, also profoundly attractive. Here is a witness of firm faith in the God of mercy. This is the God Who calls us to His side so He may comfort us as He lifts us up. This too is an example of how God will never fail to bring good out of evil when we turn to Him with confident hope.

Because of this very fact, darkness and sin want to keep us in despair, and as we age we can learn how to torture ourselves with all kinds of condemnation and doubt. Sinful anger is a popular choice. Being able to tell the difference between righteous and sinful anger comes with prayer and counsel. If you don't want to use these filters, chances are good there's a sinful form of anger afoot.

Sinful anger is a hook to hang our hatred on. In Dante's trilogy, those who walk the hills of Purgatory in need of repentance for their sins of anger sing their petitions to the Lamb once slain: *"Lamb of God Who takes away the sins of the world, have mercy on us."* During my days of raw rage, I would silently repeat this plea to the Lamb, picturing the words wrapping around my shoulders as a shield against the terrible taunts of condemning anger.

Sins of anger distort our judgment. Those who persist in this sin until death, Dante imagines in Hell, accompanied by their *"suffocating vice."* He portrays them as creatures buried up to their mouths in mud. As much as the offender may deny his actions, he too suffers from self-loathing and rage. Since the offenders' crime is based in a need for power, their anger often translates into control and domination. *"The way to have control, they think, is to have it over others; it's effective,"* Salkeld says. Can peace ever be restored to such people or to those they hurt? The obstacles are strong lies.

Salkeld explains that the inmates she works with are spiritually broken as children, so many can't make sense of the depth of their crimes against others. "Only some of them will respond to the spiritual component," she notes.

"They don't believe (in spirituality) because they don't see it, she continued. Some are limited cognitively. They can't grasp it. Having a soul? They know they have a body and they have learned to use it because it's been violated. They've learned that's all there is. They're not able to see past that. That's why the hold is so strong. That's the nature of what they've done. How can you violate something if you believe there's something more there?"

The drive to commit sex crimes is a compulsion, similar to those of any addiction, but tied to sexual arousal rates. As such, it underscores the need to turn to God and allow Him to break the strongholds of spirits attached to these crimes. As we saw with Elisabeth and her father, her lack of condemnation when testifying against him (most likely the fruit of many years of prayer during her captivity) eventually opened his heart. Mercy can be miraculous.

A side note about the God Box mentioned earlier may be appropriate here. It's not to be confused with a method some people adopt of writing down their sins and then burning them up. They do this with the thinking that it will excuse them from going to a priest for confession if they're Catholic. It doesn't. There's no substitute for the great graces received in the sacrament, so don't miss it.

Forgiveness?!

Jesus commands us to forgive for the life of our souls. He knows the spiritual scourge caused by the lack of forgiveness. If you feel utterly repulsed by the idea of forgiving a sex offender, be assured, that's only natural. Forgiving, however, is supernatural. It is the Lord Who empowers us to forgive. That's why the Devil hates it. *When we forgive, the Devil comes face-to-face with God in us* and he flees. But he doesn't leave without a fight.

Ask for the grace to forgive your enemies and you'll receive it. Ask before you have need of it so you can bring it out at the proper time. Christ has already prayed that we'll do this. The night Jesus was arrested, He assured Peter, *"Satan has demanded to sift all of you as wheat but I have prayed that your own faith may not fail; and once you have turned back, you must strengthen your brothers"* (Luke 22:31–32). Any prayer Jesus offers His Father is always heard. That one had to be for us too.

We may be tempted to think offering forgiveness is a waste of time and effort. We may believe forgiveness won't change the person, so why bother? Or that to forgive would be admitting we were wrong or that the wrongs done against us really didn't matter, since we gave in with a pardon. These are lies. Fortitude is an antidote here. It's a gift of the Holy Spirit that strengthens us to persevere, especially in trial. It was fortitude that enabled the saints to forgive their killers and torturers. We can have it too.

Without the emotional release of bringing the perpetrator to court, I was left to choke on all my pent-up bitterness. Most of my non-involved family members didn't have the words to talk to me about the subject. They didn't want to go into their own pain to find them, either. No one in their right mind would, except God, and He waits for us to follow Him there, into His mind with our prayerful silence, to listen to His wisdom.

Our offender would forfeit his soul if he didn't repent. I knew it and knew he knew it. Then I'd think: *God has forgiveness for him...and I'm going to hold out?* My plan was that I'd forgive the perpetrator but he'd go to jail for a very long time.

As the temptation to hate the offender circled like a ravenous vulture, I knew if I didn't follow the Lord's lead, the impact would eventually destroy what was left of my relationship with my daughter. Any amount of hatred held in the heart is poison. In prayer, my anxiety and sorrow stirred with hope and then desperation. I knew what my faith called me to do, and yet how could I bring myself to carry it out?

Laying down my agony at the feet of Jesus one morning, I sensed a great quiet come to me. It was vast and impenetrable. In an instant I understood what it was. It was God's anger. His anger was a silent and terrifying power against the one who had harmed His children. God's righteous, convicting anger filled me with a holy dread and opened a way to forgive. I heard in my heart the words from scripture, *"It would be better for him if a millstone were put around his neck and he be thrown into the sea than for him to cause one of these little ones to sin"* (Luke 17:2).

Even with all the destruction the offender caused, I could not wish him damned to eternal Hell. I could not. The wonderful thing about forgiveness is that, like love, it's a decision. Shortly after the disclosure, in my heart I prayed my forgiveness for the perpetrator, but three years later when the restraining order was about to expire, I needed to do more. Abject fear was again taking center stage in my mind. When we forgive from our heart, we are freed from the burden of hatred and blame. I wanted this for the perpetrator and for myself. I began to pray about speaking my forgiveness to him face-to-face.

Through prayer support from the intercessors community with whom I met weekly, how to go about delivering my message of forgiveness became clear. *Go*, they said, *but don't go alone.* Arriving in our old neighborhood soon after, I felt uneasy being there. It was tempting to slide back to the things that made my life comfortable in the past. Visiting with friends for several days, I asked each of them if they were available to go with me to see my husband, but nothing came of it. The day before I was to leave, Donna suddenly made the offer without my asking. She would be the one.

After mass the next day we went across the bay and did a drive-by past the house first. I saw what I thought was my husband's car out in front and a relative's truck in the driveway. The neighborhood was quiet on that sunny afternoon and my urge was to just forget the whole thing. We drove over in Donna's car so he wouldn't get any identification on mine. The second time we rounded the block, she pulled in front of the house. I immediately got out and walked up the driveway. The relative suddenly appeared carrying something he intended to put in his truck bed. He raised his eyebrows in surprise, and I quickly said hello to him by name.

"What are you doing here?" he answered.

"I want to see him. Will you get him for me?" My heartbeat seemed deafening.

He turned and went into the house. By this time Donna had joined me, and we stood together silently, each knowing the other was praying. Then he walked down the three steps from the back porch and into the driveway. He was bald and shirtless. The sense I got from him was the word *foul*. He also seemed frightened. Donna said later she distinctly saw a silver religious medal around his neck, but I never did. His mother was right behind him.

"What do you want?" he boomed.

"I'd like to talk to you alone. There's something important I need to say to you."

"NO!" he bellowed. *"Anything you have to say to me you say right here."* He looked impressed with the authority in his voice.

I continued. "It won't take long. It only has to do with you and me."

He seemed ready to pounce on me when Donna gently intervened: "You don't have to be afraid of anything she has to say to you."

"NO! You talk right here or get out!" He thought I'd shrink from his dare. His mother stood slightly behind him. What I remember to this day is the sardonic smile she had on her face. It struck me as odd—as though she was revving up to watch what she thought would be an exciting dog fight.

My heart beat so fast my body was crippled. I stood still and announced that "God has given me a lot of grace." I was petrified.

"Oh, He did, huh! You think you're the only one who has a God? Well, I have one too!" he practically spit at me. "So what about this God of yours! Let's have it!" He was livid.

"I want you to know that I forgive you for all the pain you've caused in my life."

"WHAT?!" he cut in. It looked like he was about to burst an artery.

Then he yelled, "All the pain I caused YOU? What about all the crap I got from the police!?"

"I know all about it. I had to deal with the police myself."

It was time to go. Message delivered. "That's all I have to say," I concluded. Turning away I suddenly added under my breath, "I wish you well."

He was furious. As we walked down the driveway to the car he decided to follow us. He called out to our backs, *"I just wanna know one thing."*

I didn't stop walking.

"Are you ever gonna darken my door again?"

His answer was our car doors slamming shut.

As Donna rounded the first corner we caught our breath. She said she would head over to a chapel in the next town. When we pulled into the parking lot the clock on the dashboard clicked exactly 3:00 p.m. Three o'clock in the afternoon is traditionally observed as the hour of Our Lord's death on the cross. In visions given to Saint Faustina, a Polish nun and mystic, Jesus revealed that His gift of Divine Mercy could be invoked most powerfully at that hour. We walked into the chapel and in the quiet, still Presence of Jesus in the tabernacle, I opened scripture and read, *"Love your enemies."*

The offender's reaction to my sudden visit is softened by the Holy Father's understanding of sinners who are hard of heart. After all, most of us can recall a time when we didn't want to reach for God's invitation to change our ways. Pope Francis assures us, "the medicine is there, the healing is there, if only we take a small step toward God—or desire to take a small step. The love of God exists even for those who are not disposed to receive it."[16]

The following day I headed back home. I had passed through the narrow gate and completed a relationship after almost three decades of loss and trouble. The peace I felt was genuine but cautionary. What would happen now? Part of me still hoped he would come to the truth and admit his guilt to the police. It was the very least my daughter deserved, but at this writing it hasn't happened. What did happen was completely unexpected, except to note that there's truth in the saying "No good deed goes unpunished."

Almost immediately upon my return, a ferocious argument rose up in my imagination. *The Devil hates and retaliates.* The first temptation was the belief that I'd been a fool, that I'd somehow given my husband power and had lost my right to fight and punish him. This was different from forgiving him in prayer. This was out loud and in front of witnesses. There'd be no recanting or explanation. Like an interior intruder, the negative rant accused and raged against the tenets of my faith. It said now that I'd forgiven the offender, the two of us must be reconciled. We would have to start again.

The thought of having made a mistake absolutely sickened me. The argument continued that if I was unwilling to take him back into my life, the words of forgiveness were a sham. When my reasoning countered that I gave full consent to what I said, the fearful thoughts turned to debasements, saying my forgiveness was utter nonsense—even worse, that I had betrayed my love for my daughter and the other victims by letting him go so easily.

I became terrified the offender would contact me, demanding proof that my forgiveness was real. I feared he would try holding me accountable for what I had said by insisting that we work together to make things right again. Or maybe, my imagination continued, he would plead for mercy and understanding, as he'd done in the past because of his alcoholism, saying he needed my help and admitting he couldn't change without my support. Evil influences relentlessly harassed my thoughts.

"In silence and in hope shall be our strength," wrote the prophet Isaiah (Isaiah 30:15), reminding me of Fr. Nortz's teaching about our imagination being the entryway for angels. Patient prayer and counsel untangled my utter horror about the possibility of reconciling with the revelation that forgiveness is not the same thing as reconciliation. When you forgive someone, you *are* reconciled with him, but it doesn't mean you have to live with them or even like them. Reconciliation calls for a compromise between opposing sides, whereas forgiveness is a loving and individual decision. "Love and don't sin" is still a sturdy guide to live by.

Some people may wonder why I forgave the perpetrator before he asked for forgiveness. It's very simple. I wanted freedom and peace. Forgiveness, by its nature, is meant to be shared. Others might wonder why I went in person when all we're asked is to do is forgive our brother from our heart. Christ commands this of us, but we can do it in any way we choose. Even though our offender never admitted the truth, I did. I wanted him to see what the truth looked like, what it sounded like, and what it had the potential to do in this horrendous situation. Maybe then he might come to the day when he'd want to find out what it could do in his own life.

The parable of the adulterous woman gives us an illustration of how God forgives. Jesus asks us for an open door in our hearts in order for His mercy to slip through. That mercy becomes the means by which He forgives. Those about to stone the woman caught in adultery are asked which of them is without sin before condemning her. When her judges throw down their stones and walk away, Jesus grants her forgiveness and instructs her not to sin again.

Don't get the wrong impression of all this. Although I pray often for God to bless the offender, my prayer is coupled with the request to *keep him far away from us.* More important, my forgiveness of the perpetrator was not dependent on his reaction or acceptance. I was doing what my faith required and doing it in my own way. The words I used did not extend to include my daughter's choices. She has her own row to hoe, and God will help her with it whenever she lets Him.

Those in serious sin don't have God's grace active in them, so it's more than likely they will reject the things of God. But forgiveness is not something we confront a person with—it's an offer. Offers are accepted or not. Making the offer is really between God and us. Reconciliation involves us with the other person, but forgiveness doesn't. It is a decision we make to follow God's will. God gives us control over how to carry it out and then confirms it in grace.

In contrast, conventional therapy seeks closure and fosters a desire to move on. There's no need to include God or spirituality. One therapist told me the reason for this is that not everyone has a positive attitude about God. *"He can actually be a hindrance to some people depending on their past experiences,"* she said. *"If they don't feel comfortable with God, we leave that perspective out."*

What God permitted to happen in my life didn't make me feel comfortable about Him, but I figured that's part of what makes Him God. There are plenty of examples in scripture where Jesus ends up making people quite uncomfortable. Usually it comes down to a choice involving a key question. There are an infinite number of situations to which the question can be applied. We are asked this question by an informed conscience all the time, but it's often ignored.

It comes down to this: *Can you still love?* Christ doesn't close things so we can move on. He transforms them, if we can believe.

For Reflection and Response ~

How do you relate to the experience of being buried alive or feeling ashamed?

Are these feelings you want to surrender? Why or why not?

How do you experience private or community prayer?

If you go to confession, how does it bear fruit in your life?

✦

 co∞

Believe

co∞

✦

3

Jesus said to her, "Did I not tell you that if you believe you will see the glory of God?" (John 11:40)

Although I was confident of God's help, things nevertheless got worse. This was a crisis of faith. My waking life continued to hammer me with questions. *What would become of my daughter's well-being? Why couldn't I see how God wanted to work in my situation? Why was this crime so hidden or flatly denied by otherwise intelligent and well-meaning people? Why was the Church settling criminal cases out of court and bankrupting entire parishes?*

It wasn't long before the questions became weights I carried inside. They created an inner negativity that acted like the father of all smart-bombs. The target was my sanity, and the bull's-eye was my faith. It came to light that hidden in my legitimate grief and anger was an insidious pride. It demanded to know *how God could have done this to me*. My reasoning went like this: if I was trying to walk in Your ways when all this happened, Lord, and now I'm asking for deliverance and new life for us, why aren't You giving me what I want?

This struggle is a classic one, and the Lord has His teaching ready. One afternoon when I felt particularly at the end of my capacity to cope and was praying my desperate questions once again, I seemed to hear in my heart, *Am I not enough?* At still another point, when remorse seemed overwhelming, a question surfaced. *Is My love not something you can give the Father praise for?* Giving praise to the Father strengthened Christ so He could suffer His death on the cross perfectly. Jesus wanted to strengthen me now, and I was arguing.

Praising God takes our mind off everything but God, even if it's only for a split second. What had gotten in the way of my doing that? Reflection showed I could give the Lord praise, but not always. Not when there was a new heartbreak between my daughter and myself. Not when I could feel her suffering and fear so strongly during our strained and infrequent phone calls. Then I remembered that *the sacrifice of praise* is most pleasing to God. So *He knows* when it's difficult to do. The difficulty makes it more spiritually valuable.

Fall in love with Me, He suggested to my heart in prayer one day. But how could I? The question made me realize that in all my prayer there was very little love moving through, in either direction. *Pain was in control.* More than the love I needed from God, and believed He had for me, it was fear that ruled. There was a huge storehouse of it inside me now. One side of my heart was full of faith, the other full of fear. Which would I ultimately give in to? Prayer would walk me through the right doors. Every honest prayer is answered. Was I really aware of the power of that? It's the power to believe.

Crossroads

Court had been my big answer. It was the pinnacle of my human reasoning on the subject of sexual violence. It's the world's solution. Finding justice under the law after a crime had been committed wasn't negotiable for me, but it also wasn't happening. The courts represented a way to get the truth out and get the offender help as well as punishment. Facing defeat on this front brought me to a major crossroad. If we look closely at our times of crisis, we'll likely find that fear is at their root—*fear of losing either our identity or our destiny*, because those are the things the Devil attacks head on. Yet God knows what He is about.

Hopefully, during your crisis times you won't do what I did, which was to spend years trying to make something valuable from the wreckage in my life—when all God wanted was an invitation to let Him grow larger in the wreckage. The tremendous fear over my family's losses made me feel protective over what little else I could call mine. This mostly meant my time and energy. So I worked a lot, and then worked some more. When I talked to God, I was really telling Him to take the darkness away, or at least to explain it to me. Letting Him *just love me* in the middle of it all didn't seem sufficient to solve the problem. Can you imagine that? I knew God loved me, but that wasn't my priority. It was escaping the pain.

Something had to give.

Inspired by all the prayer work she did with the women in her parish, Linda reached a point where she began to ask herself hard questions. She had previously believed she could heal her own past by being a vigilant mother. *"My goal as a mom was safety for my kids.* I figured if there was no molesting, my job was done." But the human solution left no room for a conversion of heart. "Some people say it's better to let sleeping dogs lie," Linda said, "and if you bury those hurts with God, that's fine. But if not, it festers."

"I reached a crossroad," she admits, "where I was faced with having to decide if I *really wanted to be healed*." As Linda reflected and prayed about her hurtful past, she saw that her desire to please God was never lost. This desire helped guide her through self-doubt and fear. The pain she carried for years had become so familiar that imagining herself without it represented a life she had no reference for, a new identity. Clinging to this familiar pain allowed Linda to stay angry and unforgiving. These feelings, although negative, were comfortable, because they were known. Linda realized it would take great courage to face the unknown in herself, to risk becoming whole. Linda doesn't make light of the work involved in our restoration. "It's all hard, but not for God."

When we feel our backs are up against a wall, we'll use whatever means are available to find protection from the pain. This may be why Rev. Bucik encourages the newly admitted inmates at Avenel Prison to get in touch with a leader of their faith group. During group sessions with the men, Bucik fosters safety by creating an open atmosphere where they can look at difficult problems. *"It's not okay not to be honest,"* he says he tells them. "To help them look inside, I get confrontational. Sexual inappropriateness is etched in one's brain. It's not changeable, but the behavior can change, and faith can help keep you on the straight and narrow."

Bucik admits there can be therapeutic aspects of the faith, but faith isn't therapy. "Our guys have witnessed being healed, but sometimes their faith is new. I question their foundation. It's got to be okay to be weak, fall, make mistakes." Christianity notes that you make errors, he says. Salvation is a process. "It's hard to come to grips with how they've hurt someone, but *what's important is not doing it again."*

"One Christmas," Bucik shared, "I asked them what they had to give Jesus, whether they saw themselves as having nothing, that they're a rat and a low-life." He urged them to be truthful with God. "'Okay,' I said to them, 'Give Him your deviancy. That's all He asks. Come to Him in spirit and truth.' There were tears."

It might be hard to imagine sex offenders with tear-stained faces, but the thought helped me trust God more. *He knows; He sees it all,* my heart pleaded with me. *Just let Him love you and let it be enough for you when He does.*

As a non-offender I couldn't make any quick connections with a peer group, but I remember meeting a handful of others at a gathering sponsored by the local Sex Abuse and Trauma Center. They were all women, mothers or grandmothers of survivors. Hearing their anger and shame, I admired their fierce love for their children and the defiance at being betrayed. I also spoke with others outside the agency forums. They were siblings, former spouses, or in-laws to perpetrators and victims. Their anguish, like mine, was a relentless torture wearing down the spirit. Relief could only wear a thin disguise as an invitation to step back into the silence, back to a half-hearted place of defeat where we would eventually agree to move on for fear of losing our way completely.

Our way to where? I often wondered. I wanted more than a shell of a life to retreat to. I believed in a God Who promises us more. I wanted inner peace restored and a return to confidence and strength. These are tall requests because we have a very tall God. Yet acceptance of the crimes seemed a phantom skill. It floated just out of reach because something kept me from claiming it. Could it be that *living in grief* gave me the illusion of *doing* something when I actually felt incapable of doing much at all? Like taking a drug gives the addict a sense of *doing* something? In reality, whether it's a dependency on a mindset or a drug, it results in a forfeit of wellbeing. When we believe a lie, we lose.

What would it mean *if I could accept* things the way they were? Would it be giving up on God? Compromising His power to save? Would it mean accepting that the often angry, sad, and confused young woman my daughter was becoming was her reality right now but it would not be allowed to take away the happy memories of her girlhood that we shared? My unremitting fear over what had happened to her made me want to sever my contact with her rage and poor decisions. Fear and sorrow wanted me to give up on her because no one can feel they're carrying both sides of a relationship by themselves for very long. But I'd be turning my back on a part of myself, and I knew myself to be completely loved by an all-loving God. Faith insisted if I wanted to love my daughter and be loved by her again, I had to live the core reality of love. *It endures all things* (1 Corinthians 13:7). Loving her couldn't be stopped by her response or lack of one. It could only get put off by my own weaknesses.

If there's no good fruit from our efforts or relationships, then what's happening isn't pleasing to God, either. By faith I knew it was time to let go and let God. Why was I afraid to do this? The pain in my heart was all I had left of my daughter. If I let it go, I'd lose everything. If kept it any longer, it would eat a hole in my soul and I'd fall straight through to nowhere.

Linda recalls her own time of intense spiritual struggle. *"Remember what we're fighting,"* she said. *"It's sin."* The interior conflict she experienced as she continued to reflect on her past and grow in faith is referred to in the Catechism as part of a true conversion, an interior penance or a *"radical reorientation of our whole life…accompanied by a salutary pain and sadness, an affliction of spirit and a repentance of heart"* (CCC 1431). God shows those who seek His will what will help them let go of their old self to receive a new one if they can accept it. Then He can do what He always does: save us.

God's Exquisite Design

The Devil and his minions take no rest in their efforts to keep a soul enslaved. This is especially true when our suffering seems meaningless to us. As Catholics, when we were young we were taught to "offer up" our dislikes and misfortunes as a sacrifice to Jesus. This personal sacrifice was something we could do for the good of souls in imitation of Christ. The practice is known as *redemptive suffering,* and its real value can only be seen with the eyes of faith. Saint Paul was full of such faith. He wrote to the Colossians, *"Now I rejoice in my sufferings for your sake and in my flesh I am filling up what is lacking in the afflictions of Christ on behalf of his body, which is the church"* (Colossians 1:24).

When I wasn't able or willing to offer God what I suffered, the result was usually a swift increase in bitterness and fear. Being fearful or anxious is genuine suffering, and any level of experience with sexual violence means you'll see plenty of it. One of the most confounding fears was the belief that the crimes had changed us from a family I thought I knew and loved to individuals I would never know. It took nothing less than my belief in an Almighty God, Who was also my loving Father, to finally convince me otherwise. Since sin doesn't change God, that meant that my personhood—my interior identity as His daughter—doesn't change either. He is all-good, and has made each one of us to be just like Himself. The meaning of my life also doesn't change. I remain a beloved child of God, and my purpose is to return to my Father in Heaven and take as many souls with me as possible.

My husband and daughter didn't seem to be sharing this purpose at the moment, but the Lord had something to say about that too: *"And stretching out his hand toward his disciples, he said, 'Here are my mother and my brothers. For whoever does the will of my heavenly Father is my brother, and sister, and mother'"* (Matthew 12:46–49). At the start of this ordeal, when I found I had enemies under my own roof, I steeled myself to become a family of one with God. Now I see that living that way unites me to everyone. My family is a multitude I've only begun to meet. The recent scandals in the Church are urging me to reach out to the newly wounded. Pastors who are shocked and saddened by the sins of their brothers in the priesthood are easy to find. "We're in this together," I assure them. The devastation on their faces and in their words is a trauma only too familiar to me.

God shows He is an ever-present help to us by using excellent examples. One of them is an inmate Salkeld worked with. I'll call him Kevin. At the start of my search for God's ways in the lives of people involved with sex crimes, I thought that if perpetrators could learn victim-empathy it might make it possible for them to seek forgiveness. It's not that simple. Salkeld knows her clients well and says victim-empathy letters can become an opportunity for the inmates to re-victimize the vulnerable. *"Many people in prison have personality disorders, and that means they don't care about consequences. This includes other people."* She shrugged, adding, *"How can they have empathy?"*

This response seemed like a closed attitude, but maybe that was because it wasn't the father of *her* child who was a predator. She leaned across the table where we sat at Barnes and Noble and whispered; *"Only a small percentage of them don't want to do it again."* My insides revolted.

Later, I figured those inmates probably think like most of us who've been through an episode of this nightmare. It's a mindset swimming in lies—like the big one offenders try to hang on victims so often, the lie that says: *You're nothing now. No one would want to know you or ever love you. You're wrecked inside.* Someone who believes they're nothing has nothing to lose.

Most of us reading this now would probably agree their view of sexual predators is close to dirt. Mine was. This thinking infused such hatred it would have destroyed me if I didn't seek higher ground. Thankfully, the Holy Spirit is always reaching for us, especially "the lowest of the low," as Salkeld described this particular group of men held under involuntary commitment. She worked with Kevin for two years before he showed signs of opening up. *"I kept bugging him. I sensed he was holding back about something to do with his mother or sister, and it did. Secrets are huge with sex offenders. It gives them a sense of power. When a secret is released they'll often withdraw or act out, retreat into fantasy or dive into work. It's depression management."*

Salkeld believed what her instincts told her about this man. Kevin was afraid his therapist might make it impossible for him to keep his disturbing secret hidden, so he used a trusted weapon, his sexuality. *"He used his attraction for me as a way to not progress."* She worked through his roadblock by persistently trusting her intuition without letting her authority in the relationship punish or belittle him. The hidden enemy was a memory of his own experience of childhood sexual assault by his uncle. His siblings had also been abused, and then the uncle had forced Kevin to rape his sister. *"It was eating him alive,"* Salkeld said. *"His therapy was going nowhere. He was in a group home and didn't want to go back. I figured out there was abuse. He felt unsafe there and got mad at me about it."* The victim who feels threatened becomes the victimizer.

Salkeld, a married psychologist and mother of a young child, had enough moxie not to let this sex offender slip between the cracks. Even if she hadn't, I saw that situation as an action of grace. In fact, when asked if Kevin's break-through might lead him to seek spiritual healing, she was quick to clarify, *"the state isn't in the business of saving souls."* Nevertheless, there was a precious save here. Since Kevin faced his truth, Salkeld says, *"He's matured. He needs to work his way out. He's blossomed."*

Consider that the above assessment comes from a professional with a clear understanding of the conviction this man carries. Yet she could also see healthy change and encourage a direction for it. As for me, I had my hope confirmed that change is always possible because grace is always given for the asking. We're free to work with that or not.

Prophecy Empowers Us

It was December and our beachfront here in Jersey was deserted, bright, and almost mild as we walked along the sand. "You're going to be so much stronger when you get on the other side of this," Carolyn said in her sunny trill. "We'll find you an apartment like the one I have. Not too big or too small. You'll see." Her words felt like finding a treasure map with only the X marked on it. I might know where I'd like to go but there was still no way to find out how to get there. But she was my friend and I wanted to believe her. Years later those words flowed back to my heart like gleaming sea glass on the timid shore of who I was becoming. All holy prophecy speaks in the Name of the Lord and calls us out of darkness. Was I really stronger? Was I finally on the other side of Hell?

How often I reminded myself pain is a natural part of the human condition—even newborns know it. A psychologist named Viktor Frankl, who was imprisoned in the death camps during the Nazi regime, saw that those who were able to survive the best were the inmates who believed that life was waiting to receive something from them. This gave them a reason to keep living. A constant temptation for me was to see my long suffering as the dismal by-product of guilt or the obsessive need to blame.

Over time I saw that pain can be used by God to teach us about living life for Him and His good purposes. This idea puts all suffering in mysterious agreement with His plans for us. It also means *Jesus is in my pain with me* and will give me the strength to bear it. Having the strength to willingly accept ongoing suffering is really the fruit of Carolyn's prophecy. It speaks of God's faithfulness to us. His plan is for us to be *strong in Him*.

Do you remember a time when someone spoke a blessing to you? Has anyone given you encouragement and peace of heart because of their faith in you? We can ask the Holy Spirit to help us look at our past lives in order to find those people. If what they gave you was from the Lord, the healing and power doesn't fade with time. We can embrace it right now and reap the grace.

Praying about Carolyn's words offered more. I learned that we suffer the pain caused by evil and sin only until we are inspired to see how loving more deeply will empower us. Since we believe God is all-loving, anything permitted by Him is for a loving purpose. This doesn't mean God *wills* violence to happen, but when He permits it, His intention is to *work through it, with us, to bring about a greater good—a good stronger than the evil.* These good things are the gifts that painful circumstances often afford, like wisdom, courage, and conversion. When we decide to believe God wants us to *"overcome evil with good"* (Romans 12:12) we have a battle plan. There's a purpose in our life, and with it come renewed hope and meaning.

Grief Gives a Warning

My daily balance of a new teaching job and single parenting a senior in high school was shaky at best. Then I got word by email that Carolyn had died. I'd had no warning except her suspicious smoker's cough and a case of pneumonia the winter before. Eventually I heard she had been diagnosed with lung cancer in late April and died two weeks later.

In the days following that news, the numbness I thought was conquered made a come-back. Insecurities about all the promises of support I looked forward to from Carolyn crashed into my fragile confidence until a friend shared an insight. She'd gotten it from a priest who counseled her after her mother's death. He told her to beware of the darkness and doubt that can accompany grief and to pray against it. Here again was the direction to pray against *negative spirits attached to a reality God has permitted.* The Lord wanted me to let a hurt bring me closer to Him.

Sexual violence isn't a natural occurrence like death—even the most tragic death. It's my experience that sex crimes have the effect of a repetitive murder because of the traumatic memories. What words of sympathy can soothe or straighten out that kind of horror? My soul was in turmoil even though I had made up my mind long ago to forgive. I still felt anger and isolation, rejection and loss. These weren't the fruits of forgiveness. It made my teaching at the community college a constant challenge. Because I was preoccupied with worry about my daughter, the students served only to remind me of where I thought she should be, in school working toward a future. Instead, she had decided to return to our old neighborhood.

"I'll just keep hurting you," she said two days after her high-school graduation. Then she left. Losing her presence in my life was like another bite of death. Yet I still believed God is faithful to His Word and never abandons us. Why was the struggle so hard and when would it end? I've learned that the fight never ends but the struggle can be given up at any time. Christ is with me and in me, ready to share my burdens and exchange my worry for confidence in *His* victory.

When I pray and listen to God, I learn the mind of Christ (1 Corinthians 2:16). The scripture readings I received right after the disclosure were consistently about healings: the ten lepers, the blind man, the Canaanite woman's daughter. While I was praying in a small group one evening, the reading about the raising of Jairus's daughter came to mind (Matthew 9:18–26). What struck me was Christ's diagnosis of the girl whom all the neighbors were treating as dead. Jesus asked them, *"Why do you make this din with your wailing? She isn't dead, she's only sleeping."*

Hearing this, my heart was deeply touched as I saw my years of grief as the wailing of the crowds in the passage, my complaining about our broken family the same as that of Jairus's community, who scoffed at Christ. It was time to look at my faith. Did I believe with my heart what I confessed with my lips? Was my faith asleep, or was it dying? The Spirit remained alive and active during my prayer time of journaling and often spoke with consolation:

My child, you mistakenly believe that to possess a faith "fully alive" is also to be without trouble and pain. Nothing could be further from the truth. In Heaven, there is hope fulfilled, faith is realized and seen, there is love abundant and ever-increasing. You are on your way to Heaven. The Way is your Savior, your Jesus. My humble, perse-cuted, misunderstood life on earth was the model of faith because I knew how to pray and how to suffer, knowing My prayers were heard and answered by My Father's Divine Providence. Take heart, Little Soul, take My Heart; let it replace your own weary one, and I shall renew the face of the earth, one prayer of faith at a time.

Prolonged grief was pushing to become permanent in me. We are what we think. These were the winds of spiritual battle Linda talked about. Saint Paul knew about them too when he instructed *"run so as to win"* (1 Corinthians 9:24).

Keep Focused

The decision to seek God's plan for healing is about you and what happened to you, no one else. To keep my focus on God's unending love for me, I needed to see Him as my Lord Who always sees me. Despite the graces I felt from prayer, counsel-ing, and the sacraments, I was deeply grieved over the loss of relationship with my daughter. These were the years of her young adulthood that should be happy and exciting, filled with promise and plans. Instead, when I looked into the future it seemed twisted in an agony of questions. Despair and bitter-ness dug holes in my concentration, chasing it with accusation and black chatter.

Another name for the Evil One is the Accuser, and because my daughter's decision-making was often troubling to me, the accusations in my fearful heart came fast and furious. It was time to face my powerlessness over the way things were without losing faith in God's power. If I believed Christ is close to the broken-hearted, then He was close to me and all those I loved.

The lies attached to my experience of sexual violence tried to harm my sensibilities by destroying my hope. The Devil wants us to betray our identity as children of a loving God. My extreme anxiety was often rooted in wanting proof of God's stake in our situation. It seemed the more I prayed for my daughter's situation, the worse things got. The bottom line was to get me to believe that the impact of the crimes had more power than God's promises of healing and protection.

Here are a few examples of the lies that tried to corrupt my thinking and the spirits most likely attached to them. The best have a good dose of truth in them.

"If you believe there can be no love without truth in a relationship, then what kind of family love did you *ever* have? After all, everything you knew about them is just part of a lie now" (*spirit of Hatred*).

"You would have suspected and eventually found out about the crimes long before you did if you had known *what to do about them*, but you didn't know what to do. To cover this up you just didn't look at what was happening" (*spirit of Guilt and Cowardice*).

"If you didn't see and didn't know about these crimes, what *else* is deceiving you? How did you ever believe you could know the truth about *anything*?" (*spirit of Chaos and Confusion*).

A basic rule for spiritual well-being is never to listen to words coming from the evil ones. The only reason I recount some of my interior experiences here is to show how vulnerable the mind can be during times of stress and fear. It's a true battle field, and maybe, some of these taunts may strike you as familiar. Unholy spirits need to be rebuked with prayer, fasting, and repentance, all wrapped in love. Without love these practices will lack power. Our struggle to resist turning toward the pull of these lies is an act of the will. We can ask Jesus in prayer for the inner strength to use our free will for our own spiritual benefit. Ridding ourselves of the influence that these spirits can bring to bear is a purification process. We want to grow in this way because only a pure heart can attach itself to Christ.

Since the active phase of sexual violence was over for us, it was time to begin in earnest again to live a holy way of life. During the season of Lent I made the decision to forgive my daughter for all the hurts and grievances brought into our relationship through her anger and fear and my reactions to them. I called and told her. Wanting to obey the Lord's command to forgive, I also hoped it would lift the burden of anxiety that was suffocating my love for her. There wasn't an outright rejection of my offer, but there wasn't any acceptance, either. Instead of anger, indifference was the new shield of choice. But rather than allow that to discourage me, I felt a personal direction opening up. I was more determined to start living the life God wanted for *me*.

In view of the fact that domestic violence is a cyclical pattern of deceit and betrayal, it's my experience that once the active stage is exposed in truth, we're left with three possible avenues to pursue. Only one of them actually breaks the pattern; the other two are spin-offs of the same cycle. Regardless of whether we were initially victims, perpetrators, or non-offenders, we can choose to be victims by remaining in a state of what Raymond Flannery Jr. calls "learned helplessness." This means we believe that because we could do nothing to alter the past, we are also powerless to shape our world now. The offender is not alone in needing to gain mastery over his behavior. A terrified survivor can also feel completely overwhelmed as I often did myself.

A second choice is to adopt the role of a victimizer, someone who puts others on the defensive or indulges in deceitful behavior just because he or she can. It's a throwback to what the active violence teaches is acceptable. In short, the lesson learned is "bully or get bullied." Survivors of rape, for instance, may be at the mercy of their repressed anger or perceived inadequacy. As a result they may compensate by dominating others or even harassing themselves with obsessive-compulsive behaviors.

The third option is to become victorious over oneself. This is evident in people who have re-established daily routines and responsibilities and can rebuild a genuine inner strength from there. Mastery over healthy life-skills doesn't guarantee successful living, but it supplies a confidence and courage to meet life's challenges without consistent melt-downs. We become the victors over our trials when we patiently accept them as God's prerogative. This kind of attitude is the action of transforming grace.

Becoming a humble victor over adversity is the conclusion of the story of Job. He went through a slew of serious losses. Members of his family died, he contracted debilitating boils on his skin, and most of his livestock and possessions were destroyed. These events deeply grieved Job because he was a just man who loved and obeyed God. Job's friends shook their heads and mutually agreed that all his misfortune was a sign of God's disfavor. They urged him to repent.

Their accusations against him and their assumption about God's judgment was another foil of the Devil. Job began to ask God why he was being tried so severely. He even argued with Him. (I saw a lot of myself in Job.) God's answer, in brief, was that He decided to try Job *"because I am God and can do what I will."* The Lord also knew Job was faithful. Finally, Job admitted God could do all things and not be hindered by any power or person. He saw that demanding a reason for all his misfortunes had only brought him more suffering. Job said,

> I have dealt with great things that I do not understand;
> things too wonderful for me, which I cannot know.
> I had heard of you by word of mouth,
> But now my eye has seen you.
> Therefore I disown what I have said,
> And repent in dust and ashes. (Job 42:1–6)

And what did God do? He heard him. More on that later; the point right now is that what I thought was God's inaction on behalf of our family was really my own obstinacy. There was a call for my life I was ignoring, a call to pick up my cross and carry it. Distracted with fears and remorse, I often broke under potent temptations, thinking that to absorb this torment was either too dire or too simple a solution. (Carrying a cross simple?) God is the origin and perfection of simplicity. He doesn't ask for the impossible. He asks us to do all things *with Him* to make His plans possible.

Deny Yourself

We become our own enemy under the influence of sin. The stronger the sin, the more we're afflicted. When a woman has suffered rape from a known offender, as in the case of date rape, the resulting shock is often so severe she is silenced. But research shows she will often date the offending man again, sometimes continuing the relationship for several months, just to find out what happened to her. The same sort of psychological hold happens to us spiritually because of serious sin. But we have a choice about what to do. We can either become dependent victims or we can do the equivalent of going to report the crime to the police: we can go to God in the trusted fellowship of His Body of believers.

Jesus is the antidote for whatever sickens us. In fact, even saying His name has power. Try it. Silent or out loud, His name is blessed and blesses us. After we bring ourselves into His presence, we can be more easily inspired with what to pray. I often asked for the grace to accept His promises of new life for me. I felt such a deep decay in my soul. Fear and despondency clung tight to my thinking. I wanted God's grace to change me but I needed courage. Part of me believed and trusted in the power of God's healing and another part saw the difficulties and darkness caused by my family's turning away from God's light. *Whenever I focused on them, I would forget God's sovereign power over all of us.* Because I'm truly without any power over another's choices, it caused an anxiety I couldn't lift away by myself.

In truth, this same realization could give me freedom instead. There's a passage in scripture that alludes to the route we must follow: *"From the days of John the Baptist until now, the kingdom of heaven suffers violence, and the violent are taking it by*

133

force" (Matthew 11:12, Luke 16:16). There are only two forces in life when we break things down to their most simple forms. Just like we teach our children at a very young age, there's good and bad. Further on in Mathew's gospel Jesus says, *"Unless you turn and become like one of these little ones you will not enter the kingdom"* (Matthew 18:3).

So often we have trouble being good adults because we've forgotten how good we were as children. Every infant is good. If our childhood reminds us mostly of negative episodes then our infancy is especially important to bring into focus. This is actually the better choice because Jesus calls us to be *completely* dependent on Him, just like an infant. All children are pure of heart until sin interferes. Getting back to that state of grace takes the work of holy violence. It is God's work in us. He places a desire in our hearts at the moment of our baptism to love and obey Him all our lives. As we grow and exercise free will we move toward Him or away. The Enemy is a diabolical intelligence ever at work to dissuade, disarm, and distract us from using the arsenal at our disposal. That arsenal is our will. If we do not exercise free will, it's no longer free. Like an unused limb, it shrivels. The Spirit advised me:

Satan uses pleasures, fears, desires for comfort, and pathways of pride to build his inroads into souls, but only through love of My will, knowing it is perfect love for you, can you slip from his grasp. Be covered by My grace and shielded in My truth. I deliver from the Evil One everyone who asks, but you must have love in your heart to receive this deliverance. I gift each soul with free will because there is nothing more loving to offer Me and nothing more dangerous to lose.

Great sorrow can sweep clean a path to great sanctity if it's not permitted to overstep its bounds. The directive that helps us balance it is to deny ourselves. Instead of cursing the dark night we find in our souls, admitting we've been broken by sin and loss can empower us to reclaim a strong free will and hope in God. Saint Paul says, *"if we hope...we wait with endurance"* (Romans 8:25).

The poet Williams Carlos Williams wrote that most of life is waiting. There are very few firsts, he says; the rest is repetition. Part of the reason for this is probably so that we can learn how to forgive and be forgiven. *"You will have to be more patient than you ever dreamed possible,"* one priest counseled me early on. That advice has never worn thin. Having patience with ourselves is often difficult under the best of circumstances. With spiritual unrest and turmoil biting at our heels, it may feel almost impossible. We can pray to receive the grace of holy violence that can help put our will at the service of God's will. It can strengthen us to make firm choices to become more generous with God and with others.

For me the crux of the problem was that my well-being became dependent on my daughter's well-being. When we are plagued by a negative spiritual force, because it is an intelligent energy it knows exactly how and when to attack us. My motherhood was the bull's-eye on my back. As a loving parent I wanted nothing short of my child's safety and health. Oppression seemed all around and God was calling me to get out of the boat I'd made of my grief and walk on the water—to take His hand and be lifted up.

During a prayer session, one of the intercessors received an image of me standing in the rain. He sensed the Lord saying, *"take off the raincoat."* Raincoats are manmade and protective. Rain is a symbol for grace. My raincoat was most likely all the self-protection and self-indulgent habits I used to soothe myself during these tough times. I took on the sins of our offender and the sorrow of his victims by letting the cruel injustice sink deep into my soul. That sting needed comfort. No one was held accountable. None of the survivors were vindicated. Cranking up a false sense of control with my behaviors and attitudes gave me a temporary but false sense of stability under the pressure of what was really hurting me.

We aren't here to live in a black hole, but to get back into paradise. It's the function of the family to lovingly accompany our members along the way. All I really had to do was give them the freedom God gave me, patiently waiting for me to look for His will instead of mine. He summed things up in this journal entry by asking for difficult but vital tasks:

Take the abandonment you feel and abandon yourself to Me. Use the shame you feel is about to bury you as the entrance to my Sacred Heart. There penitent souls are always forgiven, even those who cause the most grievous harm.

God doesn't run out of patience, but He lets patience run its course. People like Bucik and Salkeld didn't flinch on the front lines of this crime and neither could I. So often I fell into feelings of failure. *Don't let self-judgment keep you captive*, the Holy Spirit inspired me. *My love waits to be received and returned.*

Love Wounds, Love Heals

Simply being told *"It wasn't your fault"* didn't budge the pain. Fear was rampant. It followed me around everywhere, trying to make me believe I was in error somewhere, maybe lacking in faith or despairing. No, my meditations told me. *Pain and love are inseparable.*[17] I chose to be responsible to God for my husband's actions for the sake of my child so when the perpetrator denied his wrongdoing and the victims fell silent and angry; the pain became a constant inner assault. All I could do was offer it to God. When we offer God something with love and hope, He gives us back unsurpassed goodness. What was He giving me?

God wanted to show me the value my pain from sexual violence could have when I became willing to share it with Him. He wanted me to see my heartache could be a beautiful offering—and that we can't offer what we don't possess. Until I truly owned what happened, it wasn't mine to give.

How do you own a tragedy? Embrace the difficulties with the power of His grace, and that grace will subdue them. God actually wanted to receive it *all*. He knew it would help make me more like Him. Christ gave every part of His life to His Father in order to glorify Him. Jesus and His Father are one.

If the Devil can kill our desire to please God, our will is reduced to the status of an idea. Ideas can be open to argument. Maybe this was why my will to offer all the torment as redemptive suffering was quickly ambushed. *You think you can make an offering sufficient to cover the magnitude of these injuries?*

It was true. I didn't have anything capable of easing anyone's pain, but God does. His Word inspires us to believe that no matter how crippling our trials seem to be, we don't have to limp for the rest of our lives. Redemptive suffering was a tenet of my faith that went back to childhood. And wasn't it God's children who were at stake here?

The graces received through the Eucharist at mass were saturating my spirit with new life. The mass is a remembrance of Christ's life, death, and sacrifice. Read any of the four gospel accounts of the Crucifixion and you may feel Christ's anguish and pain, but equally important to note is that it was *a death He freely accepted*. Serious sin tries to confound us by saying the death it causes in us is final—but we are *eternal* beings made to live and grow to new life even through the mystery of our suffering.

All pain is made holy by Christ's share in it, Luiz Martinez writes, and is meant to sanctify us.[18] Did I believe that? What would happen if I did? There seemed little hope for goodness to be restored to my family since the disclosure, so how could I be healed or happy? But how could I be a Christian with the Almighty God caring for me and not find a way to peace? Maybe the following situation will ring true for you.

We can worship our pain. We can make a crown of it or use it like a chip on our shoulder. It can become our entitlement, a permanent attitude that says *"because I've suffered so much I've paid my dues. Now the world owes me. I have a right to rage and despise or to be revered and coddled."* These attitudes create a self-absorption and dependency that are the seeds of addiction, the route so often taken by desperate members of the three groups of those involved. After all, what is addiction if not the false belief that we're in control? As we use a substance or repeat a coveted action, we're certain of the outcome. In that certainty there's a false sense of power. That's all it takes to reel us in so the trap can snap shut.

Yet here, in addiction, is the mentality that bullies its host and foils the attempts at a loving relationship with God and others. It cannot cope. It cannot give freely. Its pockets are empty. And most of the time we aren't even aware of the burdened heart it commands us to carry. Under its yoke we lock our love away thinking we'll protect it from further pain. Instead, we become deaf to the voice of Christ, Who is Love, wordlessly offering us His unfathomable mercy.

It comes down to a war inside our will. Our will has been broken if we have been victims. Our will has been distorted if we have been offenders. Our will has been shredded by shame if we love either of them. Yet God's healing holds out a complete restoration of our free will, enabling it to be more aligned with His. Going forward from there we find we are empowered to live more at peace with ourselves and others. In Romans 4:25 we read, "Because of our sins he was given over to death, and he was raised to life in order to put us right with God." My soul was urging me now: *Don't be afraid of suffering for love.* This is walking in the footsteps of Christ. Now I see that love is really the only thing I want to suffer for. Not fear, not anger or doubt or anything other than love.

Sometimes the demand to feel in control of our emotions may be so rigid that we can't accept the spontaneous gift of companionship or support that may come from someone who genuinely cares for us. But one way we can see growth in our healing is when we no longer feel the need to be hyper-vigilant about our comfort level. We don't have to isolate ourselves to feel safe. We can accept affection when it's offered by someone we think of as trustworthy.

As we allow God to heal us, we become willing to meet others with our whole heart and mind, even those who are hurting or difficult. Because it's then that we begin to see it's only love that heals, love meeting love.

Mercy's Miracles

One afternoon, shortly after the disclosure, my daughter was flicking through the TV stations and came across the Divine Mercy chaplet prayers being sung on EWTN, the Catholic cable television station. When my daughter paused on the station listening to the chant, I suddenly said, "Let's say it for Dad," and we fell into the rhythm of the words at once. It was a piercing pain to pray in the presence of my daughter that God have mercy on the man who had betrayed us so deeply. As the years have passed, it's the same experience of pain to ask God's mercy for myself or for her. Maybe that's why the words of the chaplet ask God to *"have mercy on us and on the whole world."* Praying to the Divine Mercy that day sealed our love for God and each other even though there were many tests ahead for both of us.

Christ promises us His Divine Mercy will deny us nothing when we come to Him with faith and a contrite heart. This promise and more like it are recorded in *The Diary of St. Faustina Kowalska,* the Apostle of Divine Mercy. Between the years of the two world wars, Faustina was given visions and revelations from Our Lord along with the mission to spread an understanding and devotion to His Divine Mercy. Jesus assured her, *"You will obtain all that you ask for by means of this chaplet."* The chaplet refers to the specific prayers Jesus dictated to her for the benefit of the world.

Maybe you feel repulsed by the thought of praying for the offender. Maybe you feel an aversion similar to mine when I put on the blessed scapular because my insides felt defiled even by the thought of him. These are the times when Christ alone will suffice as a model to imitate. Jesus is a channel of mercy offered to the hardened sinner. This attitude can benefit non-offenders directly as we suffer with our survivors. There is a constant need for me to pray to love as Jesus does. If I don't, the error of the Pharisees is an easy substitute. Christ scolded them with the instruction to cleanse the inside of the cup first so that the outside would be clean as well (Matthew

23:26). This applies not only to our heart's attitude toward the perpetrator but to the misdeeds of wounded survivors *and* other non-offenders.

Jesus calls us to practice a *holy detachment*, never to be confused with shunning someone. We can develop this detachment through intercessory prayer, but even then our spiritual safety isn't guaranteed. There needs to be fruit from that prayer if the Lord is truly working through it. Am I growing in genuine compassion and mercy? Is my heart softening with hope in God's promises toward His faithful ones?

Keeping close to Christ through the Eucharist and confession and joining in the fellowship of a church community where His love is alive and active helps us to trust in the protective shield of God's love. I found that church families with a Charismatic branch often had a healing ministry as part of their outreach. During times when trauma made it almost impossible for me to pray, believing in Christ's endless mercy often defied the fear. Evidence of this mercy is found throughout the ages, and the gifts of the Holy Spirit alive in the Charismatic Movement bring us into direct contact with it today. When we're tempted to shrink from the overwhelming problem of sexual violence, a closer look at it through the eyes of faith often reveals God's mercy intervening. An example of this is the story of Debra Vela, kidnapped and kept as a prostitute in New York City during the 1970s.

As a seventeen-year-old, Debra was working one of her first jobs at a little ice cream stand on the boardwalk in Seaside Heights, New Jersey. She describes her girlish excitement when one of her coworkers, a blue-eyed blonde knight in shining armor, asked her if she'd like to go to a party in New York City and meet some of his friends. She was thrilled at the idea. She makes the point that pimps rarely look like our idea of an evil-doer or act in any threatening way, at first. They're commonly very friendly, even charming, but this is an act. Behavior that involves sexual violence on any level frequently comes from a baseline of mental illness and personality disorder.

According to research that examined similar characteristics between pimps and psychopaths, it was found that there are "many reasons to expect psychopaths to be particularly drawn to pimping activities. Interpersonally, psychopaths are manipulative, deceitful, glib, and display superficial charm."[19] These are precisely the characteristics used when a perpetrator grooms a potential victim of sexual violence. Going with him, Debra says, "was the last time I saw my job, or Seaside, or me."

Entering the New York apartment house where the party was supposed to be, Deb remembered feeling unsettled at the rundown appearance of the lobby and the elevator. When they entered the apartment, she said she knew she was out of place. She said the young man told her, *"I'm going to get you a drink."* Then, she says, *"He came back with a glass. I didn't want anyone to know I had absolutely no idea what I was doing. I just wanted to look cool and fit in. So I took two or three sips and felt my body literally just giving way. I went sliding down the wall where I had been standing and that was the last thing I remembered.*

"When I woke up, I was in another room. I didn't have anything on. I didn't have my little fancy pocketbook that I had brought. And the guy that I thought was the beautiful-happy-ever-after prince wasn't that at all. He was a pimp. He made me understand that I would die; he would kill me, if I didn't do what he wanted. Then they put you in an empty room…and it smells. And then you die. That's what happens."

This was the beginning of a life of forced prostitution in city massage parlors. Taking heroin would curb the pain of the physical beatings and terror. Deb recalled being on the street once and taking the chance of running up to a police car. She jumped inside and told the cop she didn't belong there. She knew he'd understand what she was saying, and he did. "He punched me in the face," she said. "People don't realize cops are in on it."

Her ordeal lasted two years. "You have to understand that we lived in a place that was totally sealed off from the outside world. Anything we needed or used was given to us, or not. This meant food, drugs, clothing, everything. There was a guard by the door. The women I lived with were never allowed to leave. We weren't given a reason to leave."

During that time Deb learned the games that were part of a trafficked life. "I realized that each pimp had a different personality. Some were more dangerous than others. I knew the one I was sold to was going to kill me. But there was another one who would beat his women but no one was killed. I figured being beaten, even with a wire hanger, was better than being killed. So I found out how to go from one pimp to another in order to get into a better situation. It was called Choosing. You had to find a way to hide a little bit of money every day until you had enough to sell yourself to someone else."

Once she was able to do this, she worked on gaining a degree of confidence with him by telling him about her former life in New Jersey, her family, and her neighborhood. Even a fragile trust would award her a slight increase in freedom. At first she was allowed to go across the street to the store by herself while being watched. "I wanted to convince this pimp my dream could be his." It wasn't long before she became pregnant by him. She knew once he found out about it she'd be in even more trouble so she began to weave stories about moving with him to New Jersey and starting over in a new area of traffic. She says she told him, "You could be your own boss and I'll be your lead lady." She says, "Eventually it got to the point where he actually let me get on a bus."

Once back in her old neighborhood she remembers, "the first thing I did was put my body on the ground. I was so relieved. In my mind I was never going back. I'd do whatever it took to stay free."

But her pimp knew where she was raised, where her brother worked, all the details of her old life. He would call her monthly and the threats would start again. He'd tell her to follow his instructions to meet him on the Parkway and bring the baby. "I'd agree and then put my baby in the car and drive in the opposite direction as far as the gas in the tank would take me."

She went home to her mother and explained what had happened to her and about the baby. Deb says her mother had tried searching for her immediately after the kidnapping but the police had said her daughter was just a runaway and would be back. *"That was the blanket statement they used for everybody back then.* They said I was probably sowing my oats and for my mother not to worry."

Her parents were divorced and her mom was going through a business matter in the courts at the time Debra returned. "She really couldn't handle a fight on two fronts. I tried telling her what happened but she couldn't emotionally cope with what had happened to me. *She had a lot of guilt. In her world you just go on.* She said, 'No one needs to know anything. You just go on.' That was her attitude so that's what I did.

"My baby was my reason for living at that point. It was because of her that I could quit the heroin practically cold-turkey.
If I hadn't been pregnant with her, I would have jumped off the
Seaside Bridge for sure. When she was born healthy, with ten
fingers and toes, I felt God was telling me there's more to life
than what happened in my past."

Soon after the birth of her daughter, Deb became a Christian. After trying a few different churches she says she "fell in
love with Christ" in a local Protestant community. She sent her
young daughter to private school with the strict understanding
that no one besides herself was to pick her up or have any contact with her. She never explained to school authorities about
the reason for her caution and they didn't ask.

"So for years I didn't have any treatment. I still had the
trauma deep inside. Then one morning while getting ready for
work, I heard almost an audible voice that said, 'We're going
to make something good out of something bad.' I thought, 'OK,
God. You go someplace else. I'm good now. I got this.' But the
same idea persisted over time. So I went to into the pastor's
office one day and sat down in front of him and said, 'I survived being abducted and prostitution.'

"'We should talk about this,' he said.

"'I just did,'" I told him. 'Have a nice day.' I thought that
was all God wanted. Soon afterwards, the pastor told me he
was going to have a counselor come and form a group involving adult survivors of sexual abuse. He said he put my name
on the signup sheet to attend."

She resisted the idea and then refused. He insisted. "He
said, 'Oh yeah. You'll go.' 'Oh no I won't,' I told him."

The announcement for the start of the meetings ran in the
weekly bulletin. Pastor Dennis reminded her of it. She didn't

go. The following week he approached her about it again. She finally showed up at church on the right night at the right time but sat outside the room on the stairs. "Down the stairs he comes," Debra remembers, "and he asks, 'So, make it into the room yet?'" She told him she wasn't going in. "'Yeah, go ahead,' he said, waiting. So I went in and sat in the back. There were about 10 people there, survivors and family members. No one else besides me was trafficked. It was the 1990s and it was a good turnout for that time."

The group offered a Christ-centered therapy that included prayer as well as psychology. "We were encouraged to seek individual counseling after we stopped meeting in the group, which I did. What helped me from those first group meetings was learning how to identify triggers and feelings and ways to nurture myself. I had compartmentalized my feelings and had a very strong wall built up. I couldn't feel anything. I remember at the end of one session sharing with the woman counselor that while driving to church that night the van window was down and the wind blew my hair across my face. Then I suddenly realized I could feel the wind. I hadn't felt it in years."

Those who offer intercessory prayer for the spiritual healing of others know that a person must first identify their feelings in order to be healed of the negative influences they cause. Tomas Cechulski, a deacon at Saint Veronica's Church in Howell, New Jersey, says that identifying feelings is the key to deliverance. "As much as 85% of those coming to our ministry asking for intercessory prayer end up receiving healing for past abuse," he said. He explained that "people show up with vague feelings of anxiety or sorrow, not knowing their root cause. It takes trust in God and openness to discover those feelings.

Once you do and lift them to the Lord, that's when the healing can happen."

Debra shared that in those first group meetings at her church they were prayed over for deliverance from different forms of bondage to feelings such as fear, anger, and unforgiveness. She says her journey with God through the backwater of her ordeal is "a day-by-day experience."

Forgiving her enemies is something that helped her to be free, but it wasn't an instantaneous release. It happened over time. "Over the years I thought I forgave them, but then just a few years ago, after a talk I gave to a congregation, the pastor summed up the material from my story and spoke about the pimps in a very negative way. I didn't want his attitude to represent how I felt. I felt those guys need Christ as much as I do.

"This incident made me realize that if I could feel like that, as bad as it was, with all the pain I experienced, then *those people who did it were no different at the foot of the cross than I was.* That was the biggest break-through for me."

Deb's story is a miracle of courage and God's mercy that is still largely unknown among most trafficked survivors. Restoration 1:99 (R1:99) in Washington, DC is beginning to change that. They base their identity in Christ, focusing on the intimacy of a personal relationship with Jesus to transform lives. According to its website, Restoration 1:99 says their name reflects the parable of Jesus as the Good Shepherd who leaves the 99 sheep in search of the one who is lost.

Founder Candace Wheeler explains that *"Spirituality plays a very large part in survivors' healing.* It helps them make meaning of their trauma. We are often able to help them make that life-changing connection to God." According to its website, the organization's mission is to "provide a holistic approach to aid

147

in the restoration of those who have been sexually exploited so they may live responsibly and productively with purpose, hope and dignity." Trauma therapists at R1:99 offer clinical services that assess, diagnose, and treat the effects childhood sexual abuse, adult sexual trauma, sexual identity issues, and gender-based sexual trauma for individuals, groups, and families. Through the use of a variety of modalities, survivors are helped to reduce their symptoms and move towards long-term transformation.

Candace explains, "It is very important that we do not try to 'fix' anyone, as that is the Lord's job. But we are called to be *vessels of love* so that the Lord can bring healing and restoration to those who are suffering."

Wisdom like that came slow to me. For a long time my heart—the heart of a mother—was desperate with anxiety while my daughter continued to suffer due to her need for healing. I learned most of her circumstances were textbook situations, but that only increased my sorrow. Candace admits, "Most of the survivors we work with are not ready to accept Jesus into their lives in the early stages of recovery. However, I believe the Holy Spirit works in conjunction with skilled professionals to bring about the best care for them." This perspective is clearly one of faith. Jesus tells His followers, "In the world you will have trouble but take courage, I have conquered the world" (John 16:33). The seriousness of the crimes and sin nearly devastated my world, but God in His mercy spared me. How often do our mountains of self-strength need to crumble before we can see the saving power of God and worship Him in truth?

It's sometimes the case that non-offenders, depending on the closeness of their relationship to the others, can't bear to enter the drawn-out chaos of the crime's aftermath. Instead, we'll look the other way. We may link our attitude to the bewilderment of the masses and paint the whole problem in black-and-white terms. We label the others as those *damned offenders* or *poor victims*. This may afford us a false sense of control over the chaos. We see that we can't stop or solve the painful after-effects, so we shut down our involvement because it hurts, because it's so unfair and unfixable.

But I've seen God's mercy in my situation and understand it as the workings of His immeasurable patience. He's never given up listening to me or inspiring me to offer more of my prayer for all the afflicted. He patiently calls me to a deeper conversion of my own heart. This conversion seems to be a place where there's a gate open just wide enough for me to slip through and walk beyond myself—sort of like a prisoner exchange where both parties are freed; yourself on the one side and your relationships on the other. Conversion is everyone's call to answer. As your faith responds in the hope it offers, you'll see it. When you're ready, it will be yours.

For Reflection and Response ~

Do you believe God wants to bring about something good in you from your experience of sexual violence?

What happens when you do believe this? And when you don't?

Think of someone in your life who has believed in you. How can that experience help you to open yourself more to Christ's love for you?

✦

৪০৪

Receive

৪০৪

✦

4

"As the Father has sent Me so I send you." And when He said this, He breathed on them and said, "Receive the Holy Spirit." (John 20:21–22)

After no contact with my husband for almost five years, we divorced. My daughter continued a path that was troubled and heartbreaking. It became clear that my desire to seek justice, healing, and renewal was not a goal shared with the others involved, at least not now. It would be easy to spend the rest of my life in remorse, but God is too merciful for that. Instead, He brought a beautiful baby girl into the world on Epiphany Sunday one year and made her my first grandchild.

God's grace is always available, but I need to consciously receive it. Every day I try to remember to renew my decision to accept and thank God for whatever He wills. God's plan for each of us is designed to bring about a good more powerful than the difficulties in our trials. When we decide to trust and accept His plan it's like our ticket to Heaven gets another punch-hole from the conductor. God's plan instead of mine involves a cross, but it's a cross of victory shared with Christ Himself.

So often, under the weight of fear and doubt, my prayer was mostly asking how I should pray. Daily prayer with the scriptures would open my heart and calm my spirit so I could quietly listen. My journals filled with the Lord's tender compassion: *Offer Me the sacrifice of praise. When you cannot trust others, trust more deeply in Me. When you cannot even listen to them, listen more intently to Me. If those who hurt you spend more than I give, I will repay you on My return.*

As lost and blank as I often felt, God always brought me an awareness of His love for us all. This is the power of His Spirit at work. Through prayer we can connect with God in all the different images we receive while meditating on scripture. He is the still, small voice in the wind, the woman rejoicing when she finds her lost coin, and the Good Samaritan picking us up beaten and bloody, to care for our wounds and carry us to safety. Our faithfulness to prayer can expand then, beyond words, into actions and attitudes, speech and decisions, all knit together with His ever increasing love. The Lord leans close to us from His cross and invites us to a friendship more powerful than any problem. *It seemed He was saying, See Me! Look at Me, not at what is other. I came that you might have life* (John 10:10)*!*

Rest and Receive

My mother was a retired nurse, and she was quick to say that whenever you're sick, rest is the best remedy. Rest allows us to receive. Rest gave me the first of my heart's desires, the peace of Christ. To rest and receive is about settling inside so God's Spirit, Who is with us for all time, can act in us through grace. The Risen Christ proclaimed to His astounded apostles when He appeared in their midst after His crucifixion, *"Receive the Holy Spirit. He will teach you all things"* (John 20:22).

Part of how trauma played out for me was through defense mechanisms. At first, I didn't want to receive anything from anyone. It felt safer to refuse and reject all offers. The Holy Spirit's love empowered me through prayer, however, and the faith I had learned years before guided me to simply ask for God's grace for whatever I needed—and then ask again to be open to receive it. The Holy Spirit is truth. He will never deceive. He leads us with knowledge of the truth of who we are so we can rise from the shadows of our death-like situations. The life I'm called to live is not the one belonging to the wronged wife and grieving mother but to the strong heart of a beloved child of God. Do you know who you are in the aftermath of your experiences?

The seal of the Spirit is love—not just any love, but perfect love. Saint John the apostle assures us from his experience of living with Jesus that *"perfect love casts out all fear"* (1 John 4:18). The most persistent enemy attacking my soul was a constant and varied fear: fear of all that I knew about the crimes, and then all that I didn't know crashed into fears over my daughter's well-being—and then my little granddaughter's. It wasn't my love that would overcome the fears I carried, but God's perfect love. It would remove not just some of the fear but all of it—no matter how big, how hurting, or how true.

As we live out our agreement to let Jesus heal us, we do less and He does more. When we're facing fear in any situation, the quickest, most powerful prayer is, *"Come, Holy Spirit!"* It is a call for the undeniable love God has for us. How do we let that love in? That question can become a humble petition: Lord, teach me how to pray. The Holy Spirit also guides us through the words of scripture: *"For everyone who asks receives. And he who seeks will find. Knock and the door shall be opened to you"* (Matthew 7:8).

One day while at rest in prayer with a small group of others, away from the strained relationships and anxieties about the future, I found one small place in my heart that had not yet been covered by a hardened scab. God's love waited to meet me right there. When you quiet yourself while being mindful of the presence of the Lord, can you sense how He might see your own heart?

Grace is usually invisible while it's at work. But there's another kind called *actual grace* that we can see. Sometimes God will use actual grace to get our attention about something. It was only five months after my father's death, which had been followed a month later by the disclosure of the crimes, when one of my younger brothers died. The day he passed away and the day we buried him would have been lost on me completely if not for the actual graces that showed me the simplicity and power of the Almighty's love. Remember, it's always love that heals.

It was May, and Mom had come up to my house in New England so we could spend Mother's Day together. A day or two later we got a phone call from my brother's ex-wife. Michael was an alcoholic and had slipped into a coma after another episode of internal bleeding. He was 47. Mom and I debated about getting tickets to Pittsburgh until Theresa, the ER nurse caring for him, said we probably wouldn't make it in time. She said he had gotten several pints of blood but his numbers were still dropping. We put Theresa on speaker phone and she became our correspondent, filling my small home office with the sights and sounds of my brother's final moments. She told us that she had also had a brother who passed away recently, and now she wanted to do whatever she could for her patient and for us.

We called his bedside in the intensive care unit several times that day. The last time, Theresa said she would say the Our Father with us while holding the phone to Mike's ear. By suppertime he was gone. They flew his body to New Jersey for burial, and even though he had had his advanced disease for many years, it still felt so peculiar to me that his life was suddenly finished. With the disclosure of the crimes and then my father's death, this was the third heartbreak in less than half a year.

There was a fine turnout for Michael's wake. We have a lot of cousins, and a group of his childhood friends from north Jersey also showed up. My brother had been a guitarist and singer all his life, first in a few bands and then solo when he was older. He had a Gibson guitar, the voice, the looks, the highs. In light of this, the funeral home included some instrumental Beatles music in the background tapes. It added to the contrary scene of losing someone who had barely lived a fulfilling life. When I saw him in the casket wearing a suit that one of my other brothers had bought him in town that day, he just didn't look like himself. He was slightly jaundiced and bloated, but there was something else wrong that I couldn't identify.

When the viewing ended, the family stayed behind to say a last goodbye. Each of my three brothers went up to the coffin carrying his own thoughts. I stayed last with Mom. No words were spoken. When she went up to him I was about two steps behind. Then I saw her gently push a little bit of his hair down across his forehead and smooth it. The funeral director hadn't seen any pictures of my once-very-handsome brother from out of town, so no one knew how he wore his hair. Since he was in a rock band starting back in the '70s, how he styled his hair had always been a very big deal. The mortician had just combed it straight back. That's what had looked so odd about him. He had never worn his hair that way. When Mom reached out and fixed it, just like that, my brother was back. Mom's love restored his true identity. All the illness melted away with her one move. He was lost and then found. The best part was he didn't fight it. He didn't argue or deny or resist any more. He just seemed to be resting in the arms of God somewhere.

This is how God wants to love all His children so we can live the life He's chosen for us. When we let God love us, it swings open the door through which we can reclaim our spiritual childhood. Once we do, we can't be fooled into thinking we're only a collection of the things that happen to us or because of us. We're back to being aware of ourselves as God's treasured soul.

Sexual violence carries a sack full of lies that amount to saying *"all your love is gone now."* There's nothing more frightening than that. God's grace goes right past that sack to the very center of our free will and asks us to reject it and choose Him instead. He alone is the truth (John 14:6). Some of us get edgy about accepting God and His love for us because we get God the Father mixed up with our earthly parent or a man who harmed us. When we read scripture and see how much Jesus loved His Father, we can see that we need this fatherly love too. We are distinctly made for it. Jesus taught his apostles to pray to His Father by calling Him *"Our Father."* Jesus used the word *Abba,* which means "Daddy" or "Papa." Our Father-God isn't like any other. He is our Pa, the One Who made us from His love, for His love.

God sent many excellent and holy priests to help me find my way back to God's love when I was so frightened. In each of them I could sense the grace of genuine fatherhood. When any of us are blessed to experience encounters such as these it is nothing short of our Father God loving us. God's tender care urges us to meet Him right in the middle of our struggles and darkness. Then we can receive the power of His healing in all the situations of grace He will arrange for us. Can you see those occasions of grace in your life? They may not be anything like mine, but if you're praying to Jesus for His help, the grace is undoubtedly there.

The Grace of Being Ready

Many people use various coping skills to manage their post-trauma condition. These skills include journaling, letter writing, and consistent self-care such as good nutrition and physical exercise—and these are all trusty means of support. But the most comprehensive healing requires the inclusion of our soul. If you don't feel you're ready to do the necessary spiritual work with God and the others He will place in your life for this purpose, you can pray very specifically to *get* ready.

Most survivors I spoke with went through several sessions of rape crisis counseling and then chose to stop. Years later, some still experienced difficulty making decisions and keeping emotionally stable, with or without prescription medicines. When asked if they would be open to restarting their counseling and to including in it shared prayer for spiritual healing, most said they either hadn't considered that aspect or that they didn't feel ready for it.

It takes a lot of love to look directly at our pain. Yet each of us is called to know the truth about our relationship with God inside every life experience. God is the infinite love that will give us the courage to see the truth and be set free.

We learn when we're children that God is everywhere. He's here in this crime too. Just as I was responsible for finding and following God's will before the disclosure, the same is true afterward. If I stop to curse the difficulty of doing so, the grip of difficulty only tightens. For me, a tell-tale sign that I'm not cooperating with God's present outpouring of grace is an uncomfortable feeling of wanting to unzip my life and just step away from it.

Being willing to let God rescue us from ourselves, our memories, our inclinations, is likely to feel too scary of a proposition, especially if we have sexual violence in our history. In reality, just the opposite is true and the fear is a lie. God is perfect love, and perfect love casts out all fear (1 John 4:18). Or, it might seem ridiculous to depend on God to help a person who believed his own power came from taking away someone else's. What you believed is a lie. Jesus alone is truth. But if we can ask in prayer for *the grace to be made ready for God's healing*, then that's a different experience. We can let the God Who dwells in us rise up, so we can rise in Him.

Scripture is the word of God and has remained throughout time as a loving light showing us the way to walk, but we can't expect Our Lord to change the truth. He tells us that the way to follow Him is not easy. *"Narrow is the road that leads to life and many do not find it"* (Matthew 7:13–14). If we honestly seek it, we'll find it. If we don't, we'll become lost. Whatever part of the sexual violence cross we carry, with God's help, carrying it out of love for God will bring us to new life.

Jesus tells us in the gospel of John, *"If you remain in me and my word remains in you, ask for whatever you wish and it will be given you"* (15:7). This is a large promise. What does it mean for people like us? To remain in God is to keep His commandments. Receiving the Eucharist while our soul is clear of serious sin is an invaluable aid in doing this. If you aren't Catholic, you can pray to receive the necessary *break-through graces* that will keep you close to God.

It's amazing how many of us don't pray for ourselves. We may believe that it's blasphemous or self-centered or even a waste of time. This isn't the case at all. In fact, some of the greatest saints did exactly this during their various trials. Catherine of Siena is a case in point. She spent three years living in solitude, fasting and praying in her parents' house, before she began her lifelong ministry to the poor and sick at age 19. She said at this time in her life that she knew she would need a strong self-discipline and many virtues in order to help others and that prayer and repentance would help gain these for her.

The break-through graces I needed at the beginning of my healing, and still continue to pray for, take several forms. One is finding the compassion to respect how others (in the family or not) choose to respond to the crimes. Early on, my anxiety about this was deeply enmeshed with my sense of responsibility as a parent, my authority as a former wife, and my past relationships with in-laws. With increased compassion I can accept that survivors of sexual violence (including myself) as well as perpetrators who admit to wanting to stop offending, need to be empowered, even inspired, to take on honest and loving behaviors. We can't be coerced to do so. Feeling in control is of the utmost importance to most of us with a past history of violence because of the extreme loss of control at the core of our pain. This need to control is itself controlling until we begin to be transformed and can learn to let go and let God have the control. Sometimes, deep in our hearts, we see our relationships with others and even with the Lord as an unstable or threatening force. This can give a foothold to fear. Its aim is to squelch every invitation to come and claim the spiritual renewal God already has planned. Nothing can stop that plan from happening and bringing its happiness, except our refusal of it. Have some compassion. Let God in.

Another significant or break-through grace came in the form of a gentle reminder from a friend. She responded to my fears by pointing out that God is always faithful to His promises. In the book of Acts, it says, *"believe in the Lord Jesus and you and your whole household will be saved"* (16:31). This relieved a lot of the "what if" questions I had about the future. God's promises don't tell me He will work things out my way but that He's got everything covered, His way. To let fear and anxiety live in my heart is to give entrance to false gods. I must be diligent in prayer against this. Here is part of the beauty of reaching out to those we trust. All those who believe are potential team-players. We can ask for their prayers and offer them our own.

Sometimes a survivor receives the grace of being ready unexpectedly, as in the case of Matthew Sandusky. He was initially slated to testify for the defense in the sex-abuse case against his father, Jerry, a former assistant coach at Penn State University. Then Matthew turned up as a surprise witness for the prosecution when he disclosed his own childhood abuse perpetrated by his father. He said the witness of other survivors strengthened him enough to decide that he didn't want his father to be acquitted and remain at risk for harming others.

There are also instances where survivors are empowered to seek personal change, but they're detoured because significant others can't follow suit. Spouses, siblings, parents, and friends of survivors often suffer emotions similar to those of the primary victim, but their ideas and decisions about prosecution or counseling may differ greatly. This can increase the negativity in the situation, and bring about a sense of overall hopelessness about the value and purpose of a relationship.

This is what almost happened between Ellen and her parents. Growing up with an alcoholic father and a mother who eventually divorced him, Ellen became a victim of domestic violence as a young adult living with abusive boyfriends. After several months of out-patient therapy following a near-fatal episode at the hands of her last partner, Ellen prosecuted and won him jail time. We met when she was rebuilding her life and taking classes at the community college where I was an instructor. She wrote about her experience of healing in one of her papers, and then shared with me her concerns about the deteriorating family relationships that came as an aftershock.

Her parents supported her positive lifestyle changes, she said, but they hadn't looked at their own lives. Ellen felt adrift in her new-found freedom and sad that she and her parents couldn't grow as a family in the wake of her recent crisis. She feared having to choose between resuming family ties as if she hadn't found a better way to live or severing those relationships and going forward without any close family. She admitted that her crises and recovery taught her a lot about herself and others. She was thrilled at finding out how much help is available if you're willing to receive it. In doing that for yourself, she said, you gain the strength to ask for more help when the need arises.

Learning this was of incalculable worth. Ellen discovered one of her chief strengths when reaching out for assistance. "I'm very hard to refuse," she told me with a grin. Eventually she realized she couldn't dictate her parents' behavior choices, but she decided to just live what she had learned while maintaining contact with them. Ellen's hope was that doing this might influence them as she was once influenced by others who did the same for her. In the end, people do what they want to do.

God does too. One thing He wants to do is show us how lovable we are to Him despite how close we've come to the horror of sex crimes. But until I was ready, I couldn't let God's love take the lead inside my thinking and emotions. Rev. Bucik says most convicted sex offenders don't want to hear about God's love either. *"'That's enough of that "God loves you" stuff,' they'll say. It's too much for them."* Taking in a message like that means we have to change how we relate to ourselves and others. Accepting more and more of God's love for us helps with everything. Eventually, God's love will grow bigger than anything else I want, no matter what it is, if I let it.

God's offer of love comes with an unconditional clause. Healing will happen in God's way. Realizing this made me look closely at how I was praying. Essentially it was a very concerted effort to persuade God to do my will. This only reinforced my loneliness and feelings of being "less than" others. It made me admit that, like an addict, I would end up being destroyed by my insistence on self-will. Sure, I worshiped and loved the Lord, but I was also fighting reality. *He* is reality and I am His creature; I do not call the shots.

The bottom line was, my life hurt. Evil had deceived me in my own household, and I carried deep fears inside because of that. Every hour it assailed me with lies that my love for her was useless now. What could be more frightening to a mother? My single defense was the truth in scripture and prayer. They brought another break-through grace: letting God be God because I am not. My daughter and I can't go back to our former relationship, but there's a new way for us to love each other. How do I know this? Because Christ promises us through the words of Saint Paul, *love never fails* (1 Corinthians 13:7–8). But does it happen by itself just because it's needed and wanted? Hardly.

Without the experience of God's great love for us right in this moment—just as we are—we can't become who we were created to be, the beloved of God. Until we let God make us a new creation in His love, we forfeit ever knowing love at all. *This is the power fear can have over us.* The good news is that God knows we're afraid and will help us walk through it with Him.

Here's an example of what I mean. There were a group of people who feared Jesus because He taught that He was the Son of God. Rather than show their fear outright, these people would often try to find fault in His teaching so they could call Him a fake. In one such incident some Pharisees complainingly questioned Jesus about why the disciples of John the Baptist fasted while His followers did not. The reply was a layered parable that included the adage *"No one puts new wine in old wineskins"* (Luke 5:36–39) because the skins will burst. The healing life Jesus offers us is new wine. We cannot stay the same (as old wineskins) and live out our healing. It's one or the other. All must be made new. My old self wouldn't fit into the new life Christ offered after the disclosure.

Yet my wounds made me believe I had to hold on to whatever I thought I could control in order to get through the pain. This only intensified the fear. Fear distracts us from faith and our accountability to God. It makes us forget Christ's love for us is invincible, and because of that love *He is accountable to us.* If you want proof, just look at a crucifix. Can you see His love for you there? He died because of it. Then He rose up again to glorious new life. When *we can see ourselves in His sacrifice*, the mystery of His infinite love will open up inside us. Then we'll never be alone in any trial, particularly those calling us to die to our sinful habits of substance abuse, temper tantrums, bullying, or any other way we sin against ourselves and others.

Jesus wants to bring us through our difficulties for a good purpose. He told the prophet Jeremiah, *"I know well the plans I have for you. Plans for your welfare and not for woe. Plans to give you a future full of hope"* (Jeremiah 29:11). He wants us to share in His bounty and holiness. It is an ordered freedom that lets us continually accept new depths of His love. Asking for the grace, we'll be ready for that.

Freely Give

Freely you have received, freely give. (Matthew 10:8)

When you reflect on your experience of sexual violence, is there anything you have gained from it that you want to pass on to others? Take your time answering that question because whether we know it or not, that's exactly what we do. Many good priests directed me to pray for those who suffered as I did, to intercede for them. This request for prayer is a continuous call that I'm passing on to you.

Sexual violence is a sin of betrayal and arrogance in need of deep repentance and forgiveness. Consent to these directives is typically in short supply. Intercession is a powerful way to participate in God's plan for others to obtain the graces they need to do His will. Interceding opens a way for me to love those who hate me or have harmed me. It teaches me to love those who cannot or will not show remorse for their wrongs. Intercession renews my sense of place as a cherished soul in God's family regardless of the alienation I may feel from my earthly family.

One night a tall, attractive, middle-aged woman walked to the front of our gathering space and posed the question, "Does God *need* intercessors?" The group became still and thoughtful under her steady gaze. Then she confirmed that Christ does indeed want our prayers of intercession. She went on to explain that when we follow Jesus and abide in Him, we become part of His life. He is in us and we are in Him. As we grow in faith we do what Jesus did and what He still does today. He *"intercedes for us at the right hand of the Father"* (Romans 8:34).

If Jesus prays for us continually, why should our prayers matter? Would it surprise you to know *the Father seeks those who will worship Him in spirit and truth* (John 4:23)? It surprised me. Our God is so perfect He *invites* us to give Him praise and thanks. He *desires* it of us because of the good it does for us. It is right and just that we do it.

This brings us back to Job. The end of the story shows us the power of intercession. After his prayer of repentance to God, the Lord asked Job to intercede for his friends who did not speak rightly when they judged that his trials were punishment for sins he committed: *"...let my servant Job pray for you for his prayer I will accept"* (Job 42:8). A humble and contrite heart the Lord will not spurn. Can I be that intercessor for those who offend me? Can I relinquish my own standards of truth and punishment?

I must.

Intercession is an offering of prayer through Jesus to the Father on behalf of others. The sacrifice of the mass is a perfect prayer of intercession because it remembers Christ's sacrifice to His Father for our salvation. Jesus is the Master Intercessor. *The prayer of the Son is always heard by the Father* (John 11:41–42). So when we intercede, we begin by asking Jesus to show us how to pray. We ask for His Spirit to inspire our prayer. Just as the trials of Job brought him to pray for those who falsely accused him, when we intercede for our enemies or for those we've injured, God will bless us.

Part of Job's blessing was a precious insight about his own life. Even in dire circumstances he wanted to be faithful to God more than he wanted consolation and acceptance from his friends. And more than that, God accepted Job's prayers of intercession and restored to him *"even twice what he had before"* (42:9). Intercessory prayer is creative, powerful, and healing. We can ask others to intercede for us until we are willing to intercede for others. We can ask for prayer to help us find our way to the Lord in our brokenness and to receive all He has for us. Then, what you receive, freely give.

Intercession gives us a place and purpose for suffering and hardship. The place is in the heart of Christ. The purpose is to witness, once more, Christ's triumph over it. Jesus is the Lamb of God offered once for all people of all time. His love as the Lamb is so perfect it sanctifies our every wound when we trustingly bring them to Him and ask, as He asked His own Father, that His will be done in relation to them. Christ accepted His cross in time and history *in order to answer every temptation thereafter not to believe in His love for us.* In just the same way, He has a purpose for whatever we suffer too.

The thief named Dismas who hung next to Christ on Calvary (also called the Good Thief) is another example of intercession. Dismas honestly admitted that he deserved to die because of his wrongdoing. His contrite heart, like Job's, was rewarded with insight and more. Dismas knew he couldn't save himself except to reach out to this prophet Jesus Who taught that He had a kingdom in Heaven. When he asked Jesus to simply remember him when He got there, the Lord lifted up His dying Body to reply, *"This day you will be with Me in paradise"* (Luke 23:43). Can we even begin to imagine how God wants to bless each of us?

Justice

Free me from blood guilt, O God my saving God;
then my tongue shall revel in your justice. (Psalm 51:16)

We don't know certain things until we have to know. The word *naïveté* doesn't begin to describe my lack of understanding about how sex crimes are prosecuted. First of all, there are many myths taken as truth. One of them is that most offenders are caught, convicted, and jailed. Stats from the Rape, Abuse, and Incest National Network (RAINN) give us the grim reality. Out of 100 reports of rape, only 4 offenders will get a jail sentence.

Once our perpetrator denied the reported accusations, I had to set priorities for my daughter and me. The short list was for safety, peace of soul, and help on how to love again. There was a list for the offender too. He needed to go to jail, face the truth, repent, and get psychological help. Wanting my version of justice kept me distracted a very long time. When family members who made statements to the police about past offenses decided to back away, the detective gave my 15-year-old complete control of the case. I balked at his expectations. But in truth, she was the sole prosecutor now.

When my daughter had nothing further to add to her original statement, the detective offered his own closure. *"He'll probably end up in some kind of jail anyway."* God knows how many other families he had said that to. A close friend told me I should demand alimony during divorce proceedings because he owed me, a lot. Still others said a win in the courts had little to do with receiving real justice. When my daughter went into residential treatment, her trauma counseling came as an added feature to her substance-abuse program. I felt this approach skirted the fact that people abuse substances for a reason and she had already named hers.

Once that reason is found, it needs to become the focus of cognitive therapy as long as sobriety is maintained. After that, spiritual healing can be addressed. Non-profit, federally funded programs can't carry any religious affiliations, so the individual is left on her own if she wants spiritual healing. Private counselors I spoke with were generally open to acknowledging their client's spirituality, but it wasn't fostered as a basic need for balanced living. It was viewed more as a personal choice.

From what I've seen, most of us aren't even aware of our spiritual wounds until we let God inside to show us. God speaks through experiences and relationships all the time. When we learn to practice sharing spiritual insights with others, in addition to sharing prayer with them, we're on our way to more frequent well-being. It's my experience that many spiritually hurting individuals are just waiting for an opportunity to be invited to participate in prayer with faith-filled others.

Even those who say they don't practice any formal faith know how to pray and are aware of its benefits.

Evil, on the other hand, wants to isolate us. It does whatever necessary to distract our mindfulness, using anxieties of every sort. Divided we fall. Yet we're designed to be whole and integrated creatures with body, mind, and soul interdependent, watchful and serene as our intelligence lights on the fields of eternity already within us. Spiritual contact with the Blessed Trinity brings our whole being into focus quickly and well.

Since the first wind of this crime blew into my life, all I knew to do was prosecute. When that big plan collapsed, there was only the God of my heart to direct me. As I strained in prayer to understand how an all-just Creator could leave us in this situation—still victims, still hurting, completely at odds with each other—it came to me: If I wanted justice, I had to be just.

The Means

Reporting abuse is mandatory in the state of New Jersey. That means anyone, anywhere, will be liable if they know (or suspect) and don't report. It's an excellent law, but do we know how to obey or uphold it? Haven't many of us been in a store and witnessed someone verbally threaten or become physically violent toward a child? Did you know you can go to the management and report it to them so that they must call the police? If you don't get a positive response from store personnel, you can get the adult's license plate number and call the police with your description, anonymously.

Most people don't know they can make an anonymous call with a report and it will be followed up. What we must know is violent words lead to violent acts. Violent actions, if not redirected, will escalate. Dire as this is, it's also true that the Holy Spirit is ever at work. We are the ones who need to keep up. God works through the system, around it, and beyond it—as long as someone is willing to be part of the means.

171

We don't often describe people as being just or unjust, so would we know one or the other of these if we saw them? The world and the Spirit of God have very different answers to that question. God wants us to arrive safely into eternal life. He helps us do that by keeping His justice inseparable from His mercy. When we believe this about Him, especially if we don't see much evidence of it, we become righteous in His sight. Righteousness is being just. It is how our call to *put on the mind of Christ* (1 Corinthians 2:16) can begin in earnest.

Over time I saw that survivors need to be empowered to come to terms with their hurt in the way they believe best. Before the age of the "MeToo" movement, most did not settle the fallout of these crimes with God or man. They simply buried it. Now disclosures are coming more frequently regardless of how long ago they happened. And disclosures to a listening and believing receiver who's learning right responses will hold out far more hope for healing than in centuries past. But solidarity and sympathy are overtures that must carry us deeper. Disclosures let others know the essentials of what happened, and knowing, in cases of sexual violence, is often made a substitute for justice. The problem with this is the knowing gets denied because evidence is long gone, and then betrayal embeds like a leech. We need to remember Betrayal is a spirit. Like any evil, it must be rebuked in the Name of Jesus Christ so we can be free of it.

Another aspect of justice is truthfulness. Working through careful examinations of conscience to see where I failed in my family relationships and taking these to God with contrition, I'm fortified to live the truth of the scriptures again. In particular, I learn how to love my enemies as I also learn to accept God's love for me. I learn it's not a contractual deal. Living out the love Jesus gives me will meet with continual conflict. God's return for our efforts in this regard is always a deeper exchange of love. He is a steadfast Friend. He listens to us and counsels us through His Spirit when we seek Him and stay free from serious sin. A pitfall I often encounter is thinking along the lines of: "Well, if I'm doing this and this, Lord, surely You'll do this and this. *It's only fair.*" No, the Lord alone knows justice and will guide my steps. I don't get to guide His. I *trust* His to be absolutely right, and not blindly, but with full consent, over and over.

At its root, justice is not retaliation but a grace and virtue. It's made of *"a firm will to give what is due to God and neighbor"* (*CCC* 1807). How does that play out in sexual violence cases? We work cooperatively with God. *He in turn gives us the faith and support to serve His purposes.* He holds that everyone deserves justice and will receive it—if not here and now, then later. One way we work with God is by monitoring ourselves. The blood guilt mentioned in Psalm 51 above isn't limited to physical violence. It also applies to our thoughts. When we desire another's harm, it's because we judge him or her to be deserving of it. To demand retribution for damages and loss is certainly fair, but the terms need to be decided by an impartial source in order to ensure justice. If not, I'll want outcomes according to my own measure, even if I'm the enemy.

God knows us well. His Spirit inspires the psalmist to plea, *"free me from blood guilt"* in order that he will be able to embrace *"God's justice,"* not anyone else's. Here is the path out of violent, repetitive sin, but we must first be freed from our own afflictions to be able to walk it. The means of being free is to offer a contrite heart. Intercessory prayer for our enemies fortifies us against the tendency to hate and want revenge even as it helps them find honest sorrow for their wrongdoing.

Repentance loosens the grip of guilt, opening us to forgiveness. Guilt and anger brought me to God's altar with a heart burdened by all I couldn't control or understand. Through the continuous grace from the Eucharist, confession, and the ministry of prayer, God showed me justice—His own kind. He gently reminded me that He was betrayed, yet He didn't betray me. He is faithful. He was judged but did not judge me. He's impartial to all. He was hated but did not hate me. He is compassionate. Negative feelings will torture us for a lifetime if we don't decide to receive what God holds out. If God's scale of justice isn't acceptable, it may be because we want it balanced in our favor. He sees all. We do not.

Supporting spiritual renewal for all those wounded by sexual violence doesn't argue against civil punishment for offenders. But since the majority of cases go unreported, we still lack the seasoned experience to see it as the next step. Even with a conviction, our human solutions for closure seem to hold sway over the spiritual. For instance, some wonder why the Catholic Church doesn't "defrock" or laicize more criminal priests. In essence, without spiritual healing, laicization merely puts a priest in civilian clothes so he can continue offending elsewhere. Healing, on the other hand, can set us free to live well again. When priests are ordained, their vows make them "a priest forever." I believe the graces of their vocation can save their souls, if they are willing, but after a conviction of sex crimes, their service in the church must be bound to a lifetime of prayer and penance.

Sexual sin, like any addiction, claims the identity of the ones afflicted. They become the action. It consumes them. This means they can't stop by themselves. They must *be* stopped. An integrated approach of separation from risk environments, cognitive therapy, and spiritual healing with the transformation it brings is bound to work best. All three approaches can still be cancelled out by an individual's free will, however. But love wins over the will almost every time. I've seen it happen. I've seen it in myself and in others. Ministers of healing first have to be willing to be the companion in the dark cave. We must let the Spirit teach us how to meet these souls along the wayside. We must pray for the break-through graces to desire to meet them.

Saint Paul suggests immoral behavior by believers calls for the offender to be separated from the Church and purged from their midst (1 Corinthians 5:11) or *"turned over to Satan."* This assumes the offender is still a believer, but sin can destroy faith—that's how the majority of sex offenders can insist they're innocent. But spiritual healing and deliverance can break through these strongholds if the person is willing to receive Christ. The will is everything. For this reason the Church must fearlessly exercise her healing gifts on our behalf.

The three groups that comprise the afflicted are in desperate need of spiritual aid and the safest haven is in the hearts of Christ and His mother. The Church must seek us out and help us become open to healing by accompanying us to these waiting hearts. Like the Good Samaritan delivered his wounded charge to the inn-keeper, Christian brothers and sisters must feel compelled to find and listen to those who walk a path of sorrow that could just as well have been their own but for the grace of God.

God's justice is especially startling in how He uses the wounded members in His own household to be vehicles of His grace. Good priests still suffering their own sense of betrayal and vexation caused by the clergy scandals remained open to sharing in my distress. Together in prayer we submitted our hearts in supplication for healing. We trusted God from inside our wounds to come and be with us in healing prayer, and Jesus came. There hasn't been a "day in court" to vindicate the wrongs done to my family, but I spend many days in the courts of the Lord with my spiritual family, who did not neglect or forsake me. There are others ready to stand with you too. As you walk in the wisdom of carrying your cross, you will grow in holiness that will make you just.

My alcoholic brother went to court and served jail time for larceny on a few occasions, and he remained unchanged—but in the end, God's promise to Mom was fulfilled. The promise told us, because of her faith, he would be saved. In the same way, going to court to secure justice is only part of the task for those of us involved with sex crimes, and it isn't nearly as easy as we may think. Prosecutors assured me that sexual violence cases are among the hardest to win. Although jail time is a critical deterrent for repeat offenses, its protective power usually lasts only as long as the prison sentence—if one is given. So if your circumstances won't include prosecution, or if the punishment or settlement seems inadequate for the injury, trust that God's justice will always suffice. And God always has the last word.

A Sin against the Spirit

We like to think crime will be dealt with fairly before the law, but often it isn't. What is fair is God's way. If a perpetrator doesn't repent, he'll be condemned. Law enforcement sources say perpetrators of incest are the least likely to reoffend once they're caught. Those who are not apprehended are most likely to reoffend, and those who rape acquaintances or strangers and serve jail time have recidivism rates falling somewhere between the other two. Since most offenders are never prosecuted at all, if we want justice for what was done to us, or for what we've done and repented of, it's God we need to turn to. Not only that, but if we know our God as the Divine Mercy, we *must* turn to Him. Neglecting this is certain spiritual death—a death that's known as a sin against the Holy Spirit.

Jesus tells us clearly that all sins will be forgiven in His Kingdom except rebellion against or rejection of His Holy Spirit (Mark 3:29, Luke 12:10, Matthew 12:32). There is more than one way to interpret what's meant by this, but in short, it means that if we willingly reject the Truth, Who is God, we choose a lie, and lies are death. According to the website Catholicdoors.org, this rejection can take the form of six different sins: despair, obstinacy in sin, presumption of God's mercy, rejecting a known truth, envy of other's spiritual gifts, and final impenitence.

Some see non-offenders as another set of victims, and in a way we are. I'm also a sinner. What constantly interrupted my staying open to God's continual healing was the temptation to despair. As much as I believed God would help my family, I wasn't seeing any of them interested in rising to the occasion. I took this too personally. Since the perpetrator wasn't held accountable with a subpoena, I took on the work of sorting out what happened in order to see God's plan for it. I wouldn't allow Him to leave us like we were. My arrogance was desperation.

This meant I had to look at the sin and the pain without letting it destroy me. It was frightening and consuming, but ultimately I found what I was looking for and it is this. Regardless of how much I love someone, I have no control over their relationship with God or with anyone else, for that matter. For someone who believed she had failed her child, this was not an uplifting revelation. I wanted to take back my power to mother and save and protect. God assured me from the start He had the ball in play, but I kept looking at the score and tapping my foot.

Each of us involved in this crime, who may feel trapped in an endless cycle of stress fueled by the obsessive need to control others in order to soothe that inner turmoil, is suffering the king-pin of human failings. We want things our way. Seeking to align our will with God's is an offering we can make daily and always experience growth and peace from it. Jesus Himself showed us the supreme results from this intention in His passion and death. When I'm reminded He wants us to pick up our cross daily and carry it, it's my cue to begin the chant one more time.

A favorite scripture passage that connects with this situation tells about *the Transfiguration*. In it, Jesus reveals to Peter, James, and John His glory as the Divine Son of God in a few minutes of magnificent transfiguration high on a mountain (Matthew 17:1–9). God the Father speaks audibly to those gathered, identifying Jesus as His Beloved Son, and instructs the apostles to *listen to Him*. When the supernatural experience ends, Jesus tells the apostles not to speak about what they have seen until His mission on earth is accomplished. Our own lives are perfectly ordered too. God alone knows the time for what He has planned, because He Himself is the fullness of time.

The same rule about time applies when we cling to our guilt and don't make reparation for all the ways it has affected us or others. Remember, contrition is from God, but guilt isn't, and so obsessive guilt can cripple us, making it impossible to trust or love those the Lord sends to our aid. "He is close to the broken-hearted" (Psalm 34:18), the psalmist writes. The light of truth will shine in the darkness and fortify us only if we consent to receive it. The alternative is to get angry or fearful and to hate. Persisting in this puts us at risk for sin by obstinacy.

According to scripture scholars, Christ showed His chosen apostles the glory of His Divinity during the Transfiguration because He wanted to strengthen them for the scandal of His cross. Jesus knew what His passion and death would do to their tender love for Him. He also knew what would happen to me when I learned about the crimes. So He created ways to strengthen me. He prayed for me during His agony in the garden. He prayed for you there too.

If you've experienced the gift of baptism, you can claim those graces that mark you as a child of God and be strengthened by them right now. Jesus knew your whole life before you were even formed in the womb (Jeremiah 1:5). He even knew that the feast day of the Transfiguration would be the same day I got married. His mercy for each one of us is endless.

God Is Bigger than the System

God's justice is perfect. When we follow Him, we become humble and just too. That's why He made us our brother's keeper. When we do all that we are able, He does the rest. Regardless of what happens or doesn't happen in court. You might think this is easy for me to say since I didn't suffer the tortures of court, but remember, at the time I felt that meant I'd lose my only chance for justice.

When courts process a criminal case, they work with proof, procedures, facts, fault, and punishment. Laws define what the court must uphold, and once it's found, or not, outcomes are decided. Many times these outcomes, especially in cases where personal injury is involved, fall short in delivering a sense of renewed balance for those affected. This is where restorative justice is beginning to change the picture. The main purpose of restorative justice (RJ) programs is to repair the harm done by the crime to all involved, the victim/survivor, the perpetrator, and the community/non-offenders.

According to restorativejustice.org, a few of the processes used in the RJ method include victim/offender mediation, conferencing, restitution, circles, victim assistance, and community service. All persons impacted by the crime are given the opportunity to participate if they choose. There are many ways that amends can be made. It's clear, however, that these practices do not act as a substitute for jail time.

Restorative justice is gaining popularity in courts and communities, but sex crimes are a last frontier for their use because of the intimate level of harm with sex crime cases. In light of this there's a modified version of RJ called the RESTORE program that was initiated by Mary P. Koss at the University of Arizona. RESTORE has delivered positive outcomes with victim/survivors of date and acquaintance rape.

There are those who think using RJ practices in any court case may return the crime to the private sector and enable continued victimization. Proponents feel that these strategies empower the victim/survivor and can change offender behavior. After the debilitating effects of sex crimes, God wants us restored to love Him, ourselves, and others. Yet so-called successful prosecution rarely leaves victim/survivors feeling even remotely invigorated or replenished.

Take the example of the highly publicized legal proceedings in 2007 concerning Catholic clergy in the Los Angeles Diocese. An opening clip on CNN's *Larry King Live* program featured a sound bite from one of the hundreds of victims, whose lawsuit garnered the largest settlement ever granted in an American court—over 660 million dollars. The woman said, *"You know what this money does for us victims? The money pays for our therapy."* She seemed hysterical, and it's no wonder. After an exhausting ordeal in court she anticipated years of grueling talk therapy yet to come.

Courts and lawyers seldom realize their own victimization by sex crimes. There's a vast difference between an impartial jury and an ignorant one. Most people either have very specific ideas about rape and rapists or they haven't considered them much at all. The fact is no one has the right to sexually violate anyone else for any reason under any circumstances. Surprisingly that simple logic is often missed or dismissed.

In addition to three of the victims from the L. A. Archdiocese scandal, Larry King also hosted David Clohessy, National Director of the Survivors Network of those Abused by Priests (SNAP). Clohessy described the crimes in Los Angeles as a "deliberate, organized cover-up" by then-Bishop Roger Mahony, saying Mahony was repeatedly informed that certain priests could not be returned to ministry where they would be in contact with children. In hindsight, is the fact that Mahony didn't remove them really as startling as it sounds? Sex offenders choose every target carefully, not only their potential victims but all connected non-offenders. Remember their modus operandi, *weak victims with strong covers*. Those most likely to buy their lies or overlook their crimes are prime prospects for a cover.

The nature of the crime is to make us doubt and deny no matter how we're associated with it.

According to an *L. A. Times* investigative report on Roger Cardinal Mahony written in 2013, he was the youngest priest to be appointed bishop at age 49 and had big plans for his large diocese. The article goes on to examine Mahony's ambitious agenda with a type-A personality to match. He'd have a lot to lose if it were ever revealed criminal priests were active in his territory. This doesn't excuse his negligence but underscores the intricate power offenders wield over anyone who knows their potential to spread scandal. Think about it. The same stronghold of spirits connected to these sins exert their power *everywhere the crimes occur.* The term *stronghold* here is interchangeable with Clohessy's description of a *network.*

The first time I heard this theory, I found it unbelievable. Not anymore. However, the emphasis needs to be on our ability, in union with the Holy Spirit, to clear out the evil and begin anew. After we grasp the shape and power of the enemy, our methods of defeating it will gain strength. And by that grasping I mean that in the course of open hearings, like the one in Washington recently between Judge Brett Kavanaugh and Dr. Christine Blasey Ford, we'll accept the intricate diabolical power at work in the devastating pain at the center of these cases.

Rape and molestation are still a stigma most often denied or kept secret in the family. Since the clergy scandals, it is common knowledge that the "family" is just as likely to be an Army unit, an Olympic team, a doctor's office, or a scout troop as it is a household related by blood or religious belief. Is it a moot point to say that I also discovered a deliberate, organized cover-up? It took the healing that time affords to bring me around to the attitude that in the end, what happened and how it happened doesn't matter as much as stopping it from happening again. There's serious injury here, and love is what can heal it. We can work toward a day in our culture when prosecution isn't all we're willing to fight for or when the last word after generations of crime is not merely a shrug, as if to say what's done is done. Injury cries out for healing and we are our neighbor's keeper.

The bottom line is some family members knew what our offender was capable of. No one went to police, until it came to my house. And I don't take credit for that—it was all God's grace. Non-offenders are only just beginning to make reports to police, not only because it's the law, but because our culture finally has the ears to hear and the eyes to see what's being reported. Our new awareness is part of the revelation of God's mercy and power unfolding in this situation. We know by faith that He has promised to make a new heaven and a new earth. When we walk in His truth, we are living that promise.

Fr. Gerald Fitzgerald, founder of a retreat house for alcoholic and sex-offending priests in New Mexico called Servants of the Paraclete, did indeed write to bishops with his recommendations to keep certain men out of ministry, but he never suggested calling the police. It wasn't done. When I heard about our disclosure, I had to *ask* what to do next. When I went to the police, I had to *ask* the detective what would happen next—I was that clueless. He had to tell me, "bring her in and we'll get a statement." Oh. OK. For centuries the common sense about what to do and how to do it in connection with these crimes was choked off by the shock, disgust, and panic at their center. Or maybe more truthfully we were silenced by shame and defeat.

Now retired, Roger Cardinal Mahony most likely knew well what happens with a police report. He had had several cases handled quietly by a local law firm. What's also likely is that he didn't know the priests he reassigned wouldn't stop offending. Sociologists have studied the effects of people's perceptions of those they relate to on an acquaintance level and most often we tend to see the best of them. Only the offenders who are convicted and receive treatment in jail have a chance for that, says the National Association for Rational Sexual Offense Laws at narsol.org, and most convicted sex offenders until very recently aren't being treated. The way the cardinal acted and didn't act isn't just his problem—it's ours.

Don't think I'm making excuses for clerics who cover up crimes. I'm looking to understand what they did and why. This will help me not to condemn. When Cardinal Wuerl of Washington denied prior knowledge of Theodore McCarrick's sexual crimes, it was crushing. This kind of revelation always is. And there will be more. I want to understand, not condemn. Do I want punishment for the guilty? Their punishment is secured. I have no doubts.

There's an important distinction between high offices and the individuals who hold them. Our priests have a vocation that calls them to the spiritual care and service of souls. That is a sanctified calling. But like the rest of humanity, the laborers in this vineyard also suffer from flaws and sins. I watched the video presentation of several survivors of crimes by clergy in Pennsylvania and my heart breaks for them. It breaks especially for their souls. The Church is not the Lord. Priests are not God. The Catholic Church, founded by Christ, is a body of believers who are empowered by their baptism to spread His gospel of love and forgiveness for everyone. May the Lord help you to come back to Him, and to us, so you can build up the holiness and goodness of His Church!

Now that cultural tides are shifting, survivors need more advocates to help them make a timely decision to report and to be aware of the likely consequences of not reporting. The longer a survivor waits to tell what happened to them, the harder it is to tell. Non-offenders can be enlightened as to the legitimacy of reaching out to social services for help on their own behalf. Non-offenders are victimized by the crimes in ways that are only beginning to be acknowledged. Hotlines help both non-offender and survivor, and now even include services to perpetrators who admit to their behaviors and want to stop them. Non-offenders would especially benefit not only by learning how to recognize risky situations and behaviors but by knowing what to do if suspicions are raised.

The primary enemy in these situations is fear that is fueled by ignorance. It's one thing to know you're supposed to call the police, but what do you say, whom do you say it to, and what happens after that? Learning information like this is a vital safety skill. Non-offenders can stand in the gap for both of the other parties and help bring about a positive effect for each if they know what they're doing and why. Empowerment of this kind can mean essential change in our culture. Let's face it, these crimes are ancient. Stopping them will call for new foundations of behavior built on honesty, respect, *and* responsibility.

Being able to make a timely report to professionals who have protocol in place is a responsible civic action. Training goes hand in hand with awareness. If we're mistaken about our suspicions, then a report may uncover the need for a new route to increased safety in preparation for the next time doubt arises. Part of our being blindsided by allegations is that we don't *expect* them. These crimes are part of our fallen nature. They proliferate whenever deviancy is left to flourish.

We submit ourselves to wearing seat belts in moving cars not because we know an accident is going to happen but because it may happen. We almost half expect it. Unfortunately, the same likelihood of sexual violence occurring between weak victims and strong covers is also true. For instance, an adult may see a child's discomfort from another's behavior more clearly than the afflicted child does. But if non-offending adults do and say nothing about it, that behavior seems validated to the child and he is put at further risk for harm. If our "seatbelt of awareness" is given a jerk and tightens up, we'll be more likely to pay attention to possible occasions for sexual violence to occur. Our culture is in the driver's seat, and the belt is tightening in more ways than one.

Remember, when we report something to authorities, we can remain anonymous. We can learn how to report by voicing legitimate concerns instead of frightened accusations. Let trained individuals get to the truth. Those in authority who refuse to be accountable must be bypassed. Reporting gets easier the more you do it. Keep talking until someone listens.

See something? Say something! This directive applied during the aftermath of 9/11 in public service messages can be modified for our purposes here. In cases of both survivor and non-offenders, if you *feel something, share something*. Often danger lurks in the subconscious or in fears we'd rather keep buried. If we can allow ourselves to feel our feelings, we can let them help us reach for help.

In addition, the perpetrator must be viewed as dangerous unless and until he admits his wrongdoing and that he is unable to stop it on his own. These crimes are so difficult to prosecute because they're wrapped in our perceptions about the credibility of those involved instead of the facts concerning what actually happened. And to top it all off there's usually no other witnesses besides those involved. Thankfully research is reporting that convictions are on the rise in some countries and recidivism among inmates who benefit from programs while incarcerated is down.

With the increase in survivors' reporting, more offenders are being held accountable, as are non-offenders who promised protection and didn't deliver. It's key to remember, however, that unless perpetrators are taken out of an at-risk environment completely, they're likely to reoffend. That harsh truth has been ignored or disbelieved for generations, and the cost is devastating.

Survivors say the settlement money isn't enough. In addition to a paid compensation, they want acknowledgement of the truth and accountability. These aims seem fair and just although not always possible under the law and with the passage of time. However, man's legal system and the cycle of human time are not obstacles for God.

Unless we explore and support the spiritual renewal for all those involved, we risk becoming another kind of offender ourselves. Part of securing justice lies in identifying facts with corroborating evidence, which as we've seen in the hearing involving Kavanaugh and Ford can be excruciatingly difficult to produce. But the heart of justice, it seems to me, lies in restoring the persons harmed. Bankrupting parishes and closing good schools due to the cost of settlements for childhood abuse cases punishes innocent non-offenders, some of whom are, of course, children. Settlement money doesn't belong to bishops or school administrators but to the people they serve.

Sharing settlement amounts with the costs of integrating RESTORE methods into the legal process would help move litigation nightmares into the light. It would pull the power away from the forces of greed, hatred, and blame and put the focus on mending hearts instead. It would be a way we can face the fear and lies with a counter-commitment—one that says everyone hurt deserves to heal, speedily and completely.

Right now the court system is our one-stop solution. We use the courts to usher those involved out of sight after stamping each one "paid in full." If the brokenness stopped there, that might be a half-worthy way to handle things. Sadly, it's not uncommon for victim/survivors to blow their sudden windfall on drug abuse in search of medicating the spiritual pain they still carry. Offenders too remain in danger. Even if they are convicted, their release date will eventually come up. Most will stay trapped in their violence and denial unless they receive the chance for the Truth to set them free.

My last visit to my former home was to help a friend with her move out to the Midwest. What I saw when I drove past my old house felt like restorative justice to me. We had had a starter home—a small Cape Cod on a dead-end street. Back then there were plenty of kids around who played together. My daughter's piano teacher lived next door and she had three little girls of her own. Across the street were two more girls around the same age and next to them two boys and a girl. Right after the disclosure, Fr. Jay suggested a mass be said at our house to clear out any lingering evil. A local priest came within a week of my asking and said an evening mass at the dining room table.

When I saw the house coming into view on this particular visit almost a decade since we had moved out, it looked as though God had blown His breath all through the place. The house and grounds seemed refreshed and alive. It was the middle of the afternoon and there was a car in the driveway just like there was when I lived there and homeschooled my daughter. There was a new fence around the lawn and a new façade above the front door; windows were open and the breeze gently pushed the delicate curtain panels in and out. Then I saw the swing set—its bright colors bursting under the oak tree in the side yard. Where we had left our sorrow some happy children had come to live and laugh. It seemed the Lord was saying, *"I never left you. I always had my hand over yours. You just didn't feel it because you let the pain be bigger. When a child walks with a loving parent it's always with simple trust. We are always walking. Do you know where? Back home...Back home."*

Receive Good News

Can we receive good news about sexual violence? Can we *really*? God wants goodness for us through the trials He permits no matter what they contain. The Blessed Mother knew this well. Every event in her life she saw through the eyes of faith. Everything. She completely believed in God's goodness and humbly submitted her will to whatever she asked of Him or received from Him. I look at her perfection and see it as light reflected from the triune God. If I ever needed help, my own mother assured me, *"Just ask Mary. She'll always answer you."* When I prayed the rosary to her during those horrible early days, I felt her compassion. When I meditated on the way of the cross it was her strength and faithfulness that lifted my spirit. She is the sinless one, and yet God asked her to bear seven great sorrows during her life. She faced each one with perfect surrender and received a perfect triumph each time.

We may wonder if she was ever really afflicted because we don't have many of her words while she lived on earth. Her holiness didn't make her inhuman but rather completely docile to God. She learned meekness first-hand from Jesus. She was His handmaid. Hers was the first earthly love Christ ever received. Hers the last look of resolute adoration He saw before throwing His gaze to Heaven from the cross. *"Imitate her,"* the Lord whispered to me in prayer. What a soothing remedy.

As you may have noticed by now, there isn't any information about my daughter's current wellbeing. The simple reason for this is that this book is about my story, not hers. But before I published it, I asked her if she would give me written consent to say what I needed to say. Without hesitation, she agreed. She trusted. She stepped into the chant of "Trust, Surrender, Believe, Receive." This gives me every hope that one day she'll find her way back to the love and joy that filled her life before any of this happened. Christ has it all waiting for her. Then she can give it to others who will flower like the seeds mentioned at the beginning. To love and believe in God opens us to receive even more of His love. It's a cyclical movement. No one, no matter what they do, can steal or kill that life in us unless we let them. She can be a witness to that truth. So can you. I'm sure of it.

We've talked about sexual violence as a crime that, like addiction, doesn't stop on its own. It must *be* stopped. And it is. It's being stopped by prevention programs that are evolving and effective, inclusive and enlightening. It's being stopped by individuals of faith and strength who turn from the world's view that sexual violence is a mired and undefeatable evil. Instead, there is a call rising to reach out and share the good news of God's amazing mercy. It's being stopped inside and outside us.

Stop It Now is an organization based in western Massachusetts that's committed to assisting each of the three groups impacted by sexual abuse. Research shows that children who have suffered sexual assault are at an increased risk for both sexual and physical assault in adulthood. This underscores the need to educate as well as heal those at risk. Stop It Now sees us as being in a circle rather than at opposing ends of a spectrum. Their programs and hotlines serve survivors, adults in treatment for abusing, non-offending family members, and professionals who work with each of these groups. Learning how to communicate within and outside our particular circles is key to understanding how to help and how to heal.

According to the Stop It Now website, founded by Fran Henry, an incest survivor herself, we can learn how to *"trust our gut"* and get the help we need from a variety of their online resources. Fran's compassion for offenders is not timid but two-sided. Her message to them is clear: there is help if you want to stop. She says many perpetrators want exactly that. Stop It Now offers practical tools to identify and stop the behaviors of those at risk of offending and lifts the communication skills of all involved to a compassionate level of sober concern.

Using their own research gathered from focus groups and online forums, the organization works to "balance the rights of victims and their families with accountability and help for people who harm children, over 30% of which are minors themselves." Working with adults and their communities, Stop It Now sees sexual violence as a preventable social problem. Their work with clients has found that adults will act to prevent abuse to children *if* they have access to information, practical resources, and support. Their website has links to helplines and common questions and answers for those who experience the difficulty of encountering, suspecting, or engaging in sexual violence.

The "circle concept" of looking at sexual violence and those it harms is a perspective any organization or institution can utilize. Seeing the crime strictly as crime or only as sin can limit us in finding ways to get the truth about it out in the open so it can arm our defense—the truth being that the Lord wants to heal us with or without assistance from the legal system. Church-sponsored marriage and engagement programs can ramp up their impact on couples when lay facilitators and clergy are informed about the prevalence of sexual violence in family histories and are trained in ways to promote accountability. The Church needs to confidently continue being a part of the solution to bring this problem to dialogue and action. It isn't merely programs that need implementing but the restorative gifts of the Holy Spirit. First you find His truth and then His wisdom regarding what to do about it.

Others in this story are purveyors of good news too. William Barker, a man serving a lengthy sentence at the Adult Diagnostic and Treatment Center for sex offenders in Avenel, New Jersey, is working out his time serving fellow inmates. I was told he works as the point man for Catholic services to bring inmates to God's generosity, and the men see that in him. He helps organize the list of those attending Adoration times as well the printing of a weekly bulletin. As for me, the good news was finding God's own embrace after I left my home in New England. It wasn't my idea of how healing should happen, but it was the perfect way. The different people I've met, hand-picked by God as they always are, have revitalized me.

One of them is a local coordinator for New Jersey's Child Assault Prevention program or NJCAP, an educational initiative offered to parents, teachers, and students in grades Pre-K through 12. Their key focus is teaching kids that they have the right to be "safe, strong and free" because these rights belong to everyone. CAP has been on the front lines internationally for over 25 years.

Empowering kids to be responsible, aware, and capable of acting in the face of threatening behaviors by others, whether they are adults or peers, is the underlying strength shared in CAP's classroom workshops. If children have a means of keeping themselves safe and an agreement with adults to help them in that effort, crime can be quickly reported and possibly prevented. CAP also acknowledges that offenders have rights too. If bullying or verbal abuse is returned with the same behavior from those threatened by it, then everyone's rights are lost.

After attending a workshop, children have a range of strategies proven to be effective. One is the CAP yell, a loud, long, diaphragm-based roar that startles the attacker and creates an opportunity to escape. Another is as simple as having a mental list of trusted adults to tell about a troubling situation.

The next generation will be stronger, safer, and more informed about sexual violence. Because of the efforts of individuals who have suffered and survived, good is overcoming evil. Psychologists understand the majority of those who experience trauma from life events such as sexual violence do find their footing again if they receive treatment and support. Successful survivors have certain attitudes in common. Among them is a willingness to feel their feelings, stay connected with their community rather than withdraw, deepen their spirituality, and take a new direction in life. In short, they allow themselves to be transformed.

Does that sound familiar? It's been God's plan for us all along. We hear only a fraction of the many stories about the people who come out stronger on the other side of sexual violence. In fact, there's more data showing the life-long negative effects. Linda Whalen knows differently. Instead of a survivor she calls herself "a restored child of God." Will you be one too?

Nicole is. So are her four children. During her prolonged court battle, Nicole worked with the state's Coalition Against Domestic Violence to change visitation laws and increase safety between children and a separated parent who is suspected of offending. As her disgracefully prolonged court case came to a close after nearly five years, Nicole was exhausted and disillusioned. She felt forced into accepting a plea-bargain that denied her husband all parental rights to each of their four children in exchange for no time behind bars.

On the last day in court, empowered by the Spirit, Nicole read aloud a letter she'd written to her former husband in his presence. It put on record the details of her debilitating ordeal before and since her son's disclosure. The letter expressed her feelings in regard to the injuries her children suffered as well as her grief from the experience of personal trauma.

The three older children (still in grammar school at the time) also took advantage of their right to exercise restorative justice practices. Her third child Danny, now age eight, read his own letter to his father. Nicole's daughter wrote a letter that was read aloud. Her oldest son, who chose not to appear in court, was granted his request for a full name change. Not only did he switch his last name to Nicole's maiden name as was the case with his siblings, but he changed his first name, too. At birth he had been named after his father, but now he chose to begin a new life with a completely new name. Saint Paul writes in a letter to the Romans, *"be transformed by the renewal of your mind"* (Romans 12:20). When the Holy Spirit can slow us down and ease us through the pain of our dilemmas, His inspiration can take us places in our hearts and minds that we've never imagined. Give in to God's timing. He's never in hurry but always does all things well.

Who could have guessed that a woman who found her freedom after being trafficked for sex would want to become a lifeline for current victims? That's exactly what Debra Vela is doing. "For the longest time my past experience of being trafficked made me feel I'd rather be dead than to have to carry the pain of it every day. Dying looked easier." But once she found a life in God, her perspective changed. She says a piece of scripture that inspires her is from Romans 12. "Do not repay anyone evil for evil; be concerned for what is noble in the sight of all. If possible, on your part, live at peace with all."

Vela offers qualified assistance to trafficked victims, including networking contacts for tattoo removal, her informed, personal counsel from a peer perspective, and *Ride Outs* or prearranged transports to safe spaces. She says there's certain criteria to schedule a transportation appointment and these are discussed with her via email. Her contact information is listed with the resources here.

The Sunday after New Year's Day is known as Epiphany Sunday in the Catholic Church. It celebrates the Epiphany or manifestation of the Lord to the visiting Magi. As I mentioned earlier, it was on this wonderful day a wonderful baby girl was born, and my wonderful daughter became a mother. God made

His Presence known to all of us in the joyous being of this lovely child. She grows sweeter and more precious with every year.

Unfortunately, her mom and dad were not able to work out a successful marriage and separated before the little girl was three. It broke everyone's heart, especially the little girl's, because it was decided that she would live primarily with her dad. She was too little to understand why. Her dad loves her, of course, but she was lost without her mother. That's when she and I came to know each other better, thanks to the efforts of her father. With the frightened sadness we carried in our hearts for a person we both loved who couldn't be with us, a bridge was built.

This incredible girl (I call her my Greatest Girl) came to visit me several times at the Jersey Shore during the summers she was three, four, and five years old. Slowly, quietly, we learned it was okay to talk about what hurt us inside and who we missed and what we could do about it. She needed me to be strong, to open myself, and risk facing with her the hurt she had—eventually seeing it was my hurt too. She was my reason to try to love someone again. She needed to be loved and she innocently showed me that the broken love I had left to give would be just fine with her. She likes to read a book I had gotten for her mom years ago. It's called *The Hug Book*, and we walk to the bakery around the corner—just as I used to with my daughter—and I let her pick out a gigantic cookie with sprinkles on top. For me, holding her hand as we walk down the street is one of the most wonderful moments of all.

It was a summer night before school started when it happened. The little girl wanted to sleep in my bed with me because she was really missing her mom. So we were sleeping side by side when suddenly the little girl started kicking her legs and sat up, asking in a sleepy moan, *"Is it real?"* Then with half a cry she asked again. *"Is it?"*

"What, honey? Is what real?" Now I was fully awake.

"Jesus. Is He real?"

"Oh, yes!" I answered. "He's very real!"

I couldn't imagine what was going on with her. Was she talking in her sleep? Then she said, *"And does Mary have lambs too?"*

"Yes, sweetheart, yes, Mary has lambs like you and me."

Then I remembered that right above my bed was an old, framed line drawing of the Good Shepherd holding His beloved sheep. It had been in our family for generations. The little girl used to look at it intently sometimes but had never said anything about it before. I gave her a hug and she lay back down, sleepy and still. Unless you turn and become like one of these, you shall not enter the kingdom (Matthew 18:3).

This little girl's love reached right through every fear she had because it was perfect. Her restless dreaming woke her and gave her an urgent question—the one we all carry. This little girl's perfect love moved aside all my frightening loss and filled my heart instead with strength and faith. Calming her fears that night seemed to change my sorrow and the fallout from its countless after-shocks into a bright and humble force. It told me that my heart would always be able to love, no matter what. And that meant I could receive love too. God's Holy Spirit has a plan for each of us to receive His perfect love. Find yours. It's real.

For Reflection and Response ~

As you are healing, what do you want to receive most from God?

What do you think God wants to receive most from you?

What actions do you need to take to bring these things about?

Arise ~ An Epilogue

Our person exists only because You do, Lord.
If we've been shattered by experiences, it doesn't change You.
Therefore, we can always become whole again.

"There are some things we just can't know now," my mother would often say. That maxim fits well with the memory of a time when my daughter might have come close to telling me what was happening to her, but she didn't.

It was when the two of us went to an all-day Al-Anon seminar for families. She was 11 or 12 at the time. During the lunch break we sat by ourselves on the ledge of a stage in the large auditorium of the school building that was hosting the event. I shared with her some information from the last talk I attended and mentioned that the topic was the wide-reaching effects on the family when it involves an active alcoholic. Some participants, I told her, said verbal, physical, and other types of abuse often happen. She stopped eating her sandwich. Then I asked, *"Did Daddy ever do anything to hurt you that you know is wrong to do?"*

She sat very still and said nothing. I continued, "If anything ever happens between you and Dad, you must tell me. You must. Do you understand?" She nodded in silence.

What I know now about that incident is far more than what I knew then.

A survivor or a witness to a sexual crime may only become willing to tell what they know if they believe the person available to hear them will be capable of getting the help they need. Sexual violence is troubling on many levels, and the persons involved are often terrified and deeply confused by that trouble. They need to feel safe enough to become *willing* to tell. Non-offenders share that fear from another angle. If we suspect something, we need to act. If we don't know what to do or are afraid to do what we're supposed to, we often shut down so suspicion won't rock our inner boat.

If my daughter had told me that afternoon at the conference, all I would have known to do then would have been to confront my husband, causing an instant war. Instead, God had the perfect storm perfectly planned that put Fr. Jay in the mix and all the other help we received. As much as I would have wanted her to trust me and tell me, she knew somehow that at that time, I couldn't be the one.

Over time I realized that because I didn't know a safe course of action to take with a disclosure, I subconsciously turned away from becoming aware or *willing* to believe that it could be a possibility. This has taught me that we must pay attention to what we fear. If we can direct fear (instead of being bullied by it) toward avenues of help, it won't steal our freedom to act in the right way.

Listening to a child or an adult talk about their experience of sexual violence is only a foundational form of respect, and it's tough enough. But disclosures about sex crimes can be so uncomfortable or frightening that we often feel compelled to shove them back at the speaker with our silence or outrage. With the recent cultural changes in our country, conversations of this kind are opening up and discussion is beginning to flow.

For instance, voices in the media are asking, What can men do about this problem? That's a good place to start, but involving non-offenders as a whole would unite a much larger group. The short answer seems to be we can arm ourselves with encouragement and gratitude that a survivor chose to speak to us in order to get help. We can assure them they deserve every kindness and that there are many good people to contact who are capable of helping them. An effective response to a disclosure is becoming more doable every day. We don't have to judge or solve anything. We do need to try to understand. When an offender tells us he wants to stop or that he's being falsely accused, we need to listen and direct him to help. This cuts the fear factor considerably. God will not abandon His people.

Knowing how to do the next right thing such as offering referrals or accompanying those involved to obtain further help isn't an impossible task, it's a loving obligation. If we don't have access to these resources we can find someone who does. Are you willing to hear someone tell you what happened to them and meet the shock of it with compassion? I'm sure you can be. Our will is everything.

A friend told me once that the truth goes through different sieves. I've never struggled to know the truth more than in the backwater of this experience. Knowing the truth about my family took everything away and then gave it all back with one major difference. When I see the Truth as the Person of Jesus Christ, it means I have all the help I need to do the most loving thing in response to what happened—and to all that ever will happen. And that's all there is to do about anything. The confounding panic stops there. Jesus, as they say, is the answer.

Regardless of how we may feel after the violence has stopped, we haven't been left for dead but called to receive the power to rise again. This is the action of God's grace in our lives. He has a waterfall of it for each of us every day. Any lies we've lived in connection to our experiences will only have power if we continue to believe them. For me, one of the most destructive lies was thinking I had to live under the shadow of unending grief because it seemed that those closest to me were not letting Christ help them heal. Instead of grief there is the truth that we always have choices to make. We can't serve up healing for anyone like we would a meal on a plate. What we can do is make the offer to help and let the Holy Spirit lead the way to how it should happen.

What frightens me, in probably a healthy way, is seeing that without love and forgiveness our human brokenness will continue to cause wounds. Its aim is death to the soul. Jesus explained it to Nicodemus like this: "Light came into the world but people preferred darkness" (John 3:19). No one is ever condemned to remain lost in the darkness of sin. But each of us must consent to let the Light reign in us. We must *want* to see the truth.

The final witness of John the Baptist tells us, "No one can receive anything except what is given them from above" (John 3:25–30). When we ask for help in prayer, we'll see God's answer come through His mercy that is constant and overflowing. It will come from those around us and in our daily experiences. We have proof that this mercy is alive whenever we look at the cross. There on the cross He meets us, in the same instant we bend our will to pick up our own. It's a solitary and often dark journey, but we are promised His infinitely powerful companionship. He Who is the Light of the world, "…and the darkness has not overcome it" (John 1:5), will never fail us. Never.

In some religions man looks for God. In the Christian faith God looks for man. For all that we know and have experienced about these crimes, there is One who knows the events completely, and He stands ready to guide us through them to new life. Psalms 16 says, "Lord, you will show me the path of life and fill me with joy in your presence." As the parent of a baptized child, I promised to keep the light burning in her so that when Christ comes, Light will recognize light. My promise is sealed by God's faithfulness to us. He will help me be the best parent I possibly can. When I need strength to tend that light, I can trust His love will show me exactly how.

Prayer was the flexible remedy for my wounds. Whether spoken for me or around me, prayer gave me words to hope and believe in. As I pursued it, prayer became not only words but images offering me confidence and courage. One experience of prayer showed me a succession of images of the cross. They were made of precious stones, highly polished, intricately designed. They were brilliantly shining stones of blue sapphire, deep violet amethyst, ruby, garnet, opal, and topaz gold. These images remind me that our greatest difficulties aren't simply a matter of going through hard times. The journey of healing after sexual violence is not a hard time. It is trial. There is purpose and meaning in it, God's purpose. Let Him show you what He sees and what He wants to bring from your trials. Know that as you say yes to Him and wait with trust, His response will always bring goodness. This was true thousands of years ago and it's true now. The stories here are only an intro to your own. May God bless you with His gifts of faith, peace and protection.

> She preserved him from foes,
> and secured him against ambush.
> And she gave him the prize for his stern struggle
> that he might know that devotion to God
> is mightier than all else. (Wisdom 10:12)

For Reflection and Response ~

Healing is a forward-moving force. This means it will meet with resistance. During your prayer, can you identify any spirits not of God that may hinder your spiritual renewal?

Are you open to becoming more joyful as you grow into God's plan for your healing?

If not, what are the obstacles to your having a joyful future?

How do you see God helping you overcome these obstacles?

Do you have any good news about this subject you can share with others?

THE GOOD SHEPHERD

The Association of Our Blessed Lady of Victory

Notes

[1] https://christianhistoryinstitute.org/incontext/article/julian.

[2] "Church allowed abuse by priest for years" Jan. 6, 2002, Spotlight Investigations, www.boston.com.

[3] Bill Anderson, *When Child Abuse Comes to Church*, pp. 51–62, Bethany House Publishers, 1992.

[4] Andrea Agardy, "After sex incidents, parents urge board to change notification policy," *The Ocean Star*, 31 March, 2006, pp. 3, 17.

[5] Lauren N. Akins, "Fired teacher admits to affair with student," *The Ocean Star*, April 28, 2006, pp. 1, 18.

[6] "Josef Fritzl admits all charges," www.bbc.com, March 18, 2009, BBC 2015.

[7] Catholicdigest.com, "Discover the secrets of the scapular," Karen Edmisten, March 2009.

[8] *Healing Life's Deepest Hurts*, Edward M. Smith, Servant Publications and New Creation Publishing, 2002, pp. 11–17.

[9] Michael Bradley, *Interpretation of Matthew 12:45—Demons*, www.bible-knowledge.com.

[10] Robert Frost, *Snow*. 1920. Bartelby.com.

[11] Fr. Basil Nortz, ORC. *On Holy Silence/Twelve forms of silence*. Three conferences, Los Angeles, CA. Sept. 1997.

[12] R. Thomas Brass, "Pride and Shame: Strongholds of the Self-Centered Soul," www.jerichoministry.com.

[13] www.catholicadoration.com and www.therealpresence.org.

[14] Linda Whalen, *The Valley of Childhood*, Bright Books, 1999, p. 25.

[15] Sandro Magister, *Sin and Forgiveness in the Plan of God* by Giacomo Biffi, June 24, 2014. www.chiesa.espresso.republica.it.

[16] "The Name of God is Mercy," Pope Francis, 2016.

[17] Most Rev. Luis M. Martinez, *The Sanctifier*, St. Paul Books, 1982.

[18] Ibid.

[19] Alicia Spidel, et al., "The Psychopath as Pimp," Canadian Journal of Police & Security Services, Vol. 4, Issue 4, Winter 2006, p. 194.

Resources and Suggested Reading

Websites ~

Stopitnow.org ~ a site with abundant resources and immediate help on their hotline for concerns about sexual violence.

Celebraterecovery.com ~ a Christ-centered 12-Step Program NOT only for addictions. Celebrate Recovery is hosted in over 35,000 churches, some prisons, and other settings in multiple languages.

RAINN (Rape, Abuse, Incest National Network) located on the web at RAINN.org 24/7 live hotline: 800-656-HOPE (4673).

NAPAC.org.uk ~ The National Association for People Abused in Childhood (NAPAC) is the UK's leading national charity offering support to adult survivors of all types of childhood abuse, including physical, sexual, and emotional abuse and neglect. Their British hotline can be reached **without charge** by dialing **011** before their number listed on the website.

Fr. Ralph DiOrio healing blessing on YouTube ~ To locate his links use his name to search.

www.nami.org ~ the National Alliance for Mental Illness. Wealth of resources and support. Post Traumatic Stress Disorder is a mental health diagnosis.

Thedivinemercy.org ~ website features information about the Apostolate of Divine Mercy and Healing with links to pray the chaplet prayers.

Restorativejustice.org ~ offers information about prison programs that work toward healing the victim and perpetrator when there is mutual consent to do so. Restorative justice practices go beyond punishment, to reach healing.

Catholicdoors.com ~ a large search engine for Catholic sources, including the Catechism and writings of the saints. Both of these offer insight on sexual abuse.

Catholicexchange.com ~ multiple resources of value for all Christians.

R199.org ~ Washington, DC based center for survivors of complex trauma including PTSD. *Healing Conversations* is a powerful program by R199 founder Candace Wheeler for those in a relationship with a survivor

NJCAP.org ~ New Jersey Child Assault Prevention Program, **is** also international. Their programs empower students to be safe, strong, and free through school presentations.

Lourdesprayerrequest.com ~ a site where you can request that others pray for you and your intentions.

Transformationprayer.org (TPM), formerly known as *Theophostic* prayer. Its mission is to make transformation prayer ministry freely available to everyone, everywhere.

Books ~

Resisting Happiness by Matthew Kelly. A True story about why we sabotage ourselves, from a Catholic evangelist's perspective.

Born Only Once: The Miracle of Affirmation by Conrad W. Baars M.D. A Catholic psychiatrist explores and explains the method and results of affirmation therapy.

Divine Mercy in My Soul: The Diary of M. Faustina Kowalska. She is known as *The Apostle of Divine Mercy* because of her mission to make known Jesus's message about His powerful role as the Divine Mercy.

The Sanctifier by Rev. Luis Martinez. Inspirational and enlightening. The gifts of the Holy Spirit explained in beautiful detail. Powerful. Need help? Go to our Consoler!

Opening Up: The Healing Power of Confiding in Others by James W. Pennebaker, Ph.D. Learn how talking or *not* talking about your problems can have a profound effect on your physical health.

The Voice of Inner Love: A Journey from Anguish to Freedom by Henri Nouwen. He was a Dutch Catholic priest and psychologist who wrote over 40 books. This book is comprised of from his poignant journal notes written during a time of personal crisis.

Post Traumatic Stress Disorder: The Victim's Guide to Healing and Recovery by Raymond Flannery. Very informative and readable. A classic.

Trusting: The Issue at the Heart of Every Relationship by Pat Springle. A Christian perspective.

Unbound: A Practical Guide to Deliverance by Neal Lozano. Highly recommended Catholic classic.

Healing Life's Deepest Hurts by Edward M. Smith, founder of Transformation Prayer Ministry.

CONTACT US ~

Debra Vela: debvela@gmail.com, human trafficking survivor and advocate.

Deacon Tomas Cechulski: marysway3@gmail.com. Deacon Tom offers intercessory healing prayer through his ministry based in SC. Contact him for more information.

The author: FollowingTheLamb2017@gmail.com. Reach me to arrange a discussion with your group.

Prayer to Saint Michael the Archangel ~

Saint Michael the Archangel, defend us in battle. Be our protection against the snares and wickedness of the devil. May God rebuke him, we humbly pray; and do Thou, O Prince of the Heavenly Host—by the power of God—cast into hell, Satan, and all the evil spirits, who wander about the world seeking the ruin of souls. Amen.

Reflect and Respond

Reflect and Respond

Reflect and Respond

www.ingramcontent.com/pod-product-compliance
Lightning Source LLC
LaVergne TN
LVHW011325080426
835513LV00006B/200